Halcyon Days

LIFE'S JOURNEY

BY

CAPTAIN PAUL FLAGG

the Peppertree Press, LLC
Sarasota, Florida

For information regarding permission,
call 941-922-2662 or contact us at our website:
www.peppertreepublishing.com or write to:
the Peppertree Press, LLC.
Attention: Publisher
1269 First Street, Suite 7
Sarasota, Florida 34236

ISBN: 978-1-61493-753-1
Library of Congress Number: 2021900876
Printed February 2021

*"In order to write about life
you have to first live it."*

—ERNEST HEMINGWAY

Roberta Bearce
I have had a little time
on my hands with the
Pandemic so I wrote
a book and thought you
might like a copy.
Hope everything is
going well.
Enjoy your Halcyon
Days
Capt, Paul Flagg

Table of Contents

In the Beginning

Once upon a time, long, long ago and far away—well, maybe not too long ago and maybe not too far away, but definitely once upon a time. Yes, stories should begin with "Once a time," because if it happened this morning or last year or fifty years ago, it was once upon a time.

Time is a fascinating thing and I once heard a definition of time that pretty much said it all, which is: "God's way of everything not happening all at once." The problem with this system of everything being spread over time is that the memory cells are not set up for total recall. Even though recently I saw a television program where there are people that have this ability. You give them a date and they will tell you the major news item or what they had for supper that day. I think this is incredible, because I can barely remember what I had for supper yesterday. This is my disclaimer for not having the facts correct.

The real definition of time according to Webster's is "a particular moment," which goes with God's definition or a period of duration or conception of past, present, and future.

But how do we calculate time? *Here is where it gets complicated.* It is tied to our celestial beings, the movement of the sun, moon, planets, and stars—how long it takes them to move through the universe. *Ah, God's creation.*

With the help of the Hubble telescope, scientists of today are formulating the Big Bang Theory, which has nothing to do with the popular television show—or almost nothing.

I have studied how to calculate where you are on earth using the moon, sun, planets, and fifty-seven navigational stars and, most importantly, time and a sextant. It is a fascinating process and a great book written about this is *Longitude* by Dava Sobel.

This is not what my stories are all about. I am only trying to lay the groundwork, for they will not be told hour-by-hour. I'll try to tell them in relation to that part of my life, which will be broken down something like my childhood, while my father was in the navy, my schoolyears and jobs, boating, and retirement years. I also will talk about my love of the sea and its "many moods," about which many, many stories have been written.

Edward R. Snow was one the greatest storytellers of the sea and its tales. I only wish I had that ability. I had the honor once of meeting him at a book signing at the Burlington Mall in Massachusetts—he was bigger than life. He related that life is stranger than fiction.

As I have gone through life, strange things have happened to me. However, I just figured that my life was no stranger than anybody else's. But as I went through this contemplation, I met or heard of people who were born in Lowell, Massachusetts, and never left the city limits.

There is also the cruel fact that some people are confined to a bed or house by some fate of an accident or illness, which is the saddest fate of life. We should not be so egotistical to think that our

God is the only one. The American Indians have the Great Spirit. Then there are Mohammed and Buddhism and the list goes on. Everybody recognizes someone. I have even heard that an atheist recognizes somebody when his Creator is calling in his cards.

CHAPTER 2

Early Childhood

I will start my stories with my earliest recollections. My father was in the navy and off fighting for our freedom, while my mother went to live with her parents.

My recollection of my grandparent's house is very vague. I remember a dark living room with a piano, but I do not remember who played it. There was a large kitchen with a bright sunroom next to it and a small staircase going up to a very narrow bedroom.

On the property was a very large garden, but I think I remember this more from a picture. A hill was on the north side of the property and a very steep set of stairs went down to the house. Next to those stairs was a narrow three-story structure of my grandfather's that was built into the hill. The top floor was for his blacksmith tools, because he was the blacksmith for the city of Waltham, Massachusetts. When I bought my first house with a fireplace, my aunt gave me a set of andirons he had made. The middle floor was for general storage and the bottom floor was a root cellar where vegetables were kept.

This is how I remember the homestead of the Woodside family. However, in the late forties through the early fifties, the state of Massachusetts took the land for Route 128. Now this highway goes through my grandparent's homestead, so my description of this property is just a faint memory.

What I remember more clearly is that the state left a small corner of the property at the top of the hill. My Uncle Jim used it to keep his trucks.

The story I got from my cousin was that one day as he was working on one of his trucks, he heard a terrible crash. He had just witnessed the first fatal accident of the new ultramodern beltway that was to take the traffic out of Boston on the way to Maine.

Later when I came back from my father's in the fifties, another road was being built to take the strain off Route 128 traffic. That road is now Route 495, but back then it was called the Road to Nowhere.

A lot of people do not realize how great a president Dwight D. Eisenhower "Ike" was. He saw what the Autobahn did for Germany. When he came back after the war, he proposed the system now called our interstate. It was designed to move people or troops quickly in time of war. Every five miles of the system is supposed to be straight, so airplanes can land in emergencies. They were intended only to go from state to state. We know how this has worked out. However, each state is responsible for its own section.

My parents met through my uncle, who worked with my father and asked if he would like a date with his girlfriend's sister. I do not know any dating stories, but I do know my father's ship was in Portland, Maine. He took the train down to Boston, Massachusetts, and they were married February 20, 1942. He then went back to Portland to rejoin his ship. I was born November 9, 1942.

This information is not that interesting to most people. What is significant to my own family is that on September 12, 1942, my mother gets the news that the ship my father was stationed on, the aircraft carrier Wasp, was sunk in the Pacific. She did learn later that he had survived after being in shark-infested waters for twelve hours. This is one reason why they call my parents the greatest generation. In 2019, this ship was found two-and-half-miles down.

My father never talked about his experiences, like most men who went to war. However, there was one story that he *did* tell. The Wasp was called to the Pacific theater and told to get there as quickly as possible, which meant not going around the Horn. They knew the hull would fit through the Panama Canal, but nobody thought about the light posts and the overhang of the flight deck. The ship's captain called Washington and told them of this dilemma, so the command was to "take out the posts."

A story that comes to mind about the navy in the South Pacific was told to me by a fellow I worked with. It was after World War II. The submarine that he was stationed on pulled into a small island for provisions. They had planned to be there for a couple of days for a little R&R and a few ball games with the men stationed on the island. Even the officers were allowed to play, but one person always had to stay on the submarine. I guess a large amount of beer was enjoyed. Everyone planned to sober up the next day, but late in the day, they received a weather alert, so they had to make way. In their haste to depart, it seems whoever was in charge of untying the dock lines had forgotten to do this or had passed out. Apparently, part of the little island's docking system went to sea. Some of the stories I heard about the navy in the South Pacific did resemble the old television show, *McHale's Navy*.

After the war, my father was stationed on the West Coast, which meant many trips across country for my mother and me. I do not remember the early trips at all. My mother told me my first trip was when I was six weeks old and the only time I cried was in St. Louis, when she tried to put a bonnet on me. She left everything on the train when she took me off. I do not know where she was going, but when she came back, the train was gone and she panicked.

I guess a conductor saw her panic and told her they were simply turning the train around. It came back shortly. One story she told was where a conductor was walking down the aisle selling sandwiches. Apparently, he had only one kind of sandwich, but he called out, "A meat and a cheese or a cheese and a meat!" We weren't sure whether he was trying to make it sound like he had a variety or if he was just kidding. The answer is lost in time.

We made this trip once a year for five years. I believe it was twice by train and three times by car. One recollection was when we were going through Chicago, we were following a car that was all over the road—it ended up wrapped around a telephone pole. That had to be our last trip, because I still remember it vividly.

Another time we were in the mountains, staying in a little cabin. The strange thing here is that I remember sleeping in a drawer that my parents had pulled out of a small dresser. They put it on the floor with a blanket inside, but it was winter and so I was very cold. Whenever we stayed where the temperature could fall below freezing, Dad drained the water from the car at night and refilled it before we left in the morning.

Then there was the time we were in the Midwest—I want to say Kansas, but I am not sure. (I think everybody who has lost their parents would like to be able to ask them to recall where, when, or what certain things were.)

I have many of these moments in my stories. For example, when I was four and had to go to the bathroom—aka, to an outhouse—a three hole. My father pulls into the gas station and I was terrorized by the fact that we were in the middle of a locust infestation. I have never been big on any type of bugs, with the exception of daddy longlegs and praying mantis. I get out of the car and remember, even with my little feet, stepping on two to ten locusts at a time. When I finally make it to the outhouse and duck inside, I thought that I was out of the insect horror attack, only to find thousands of bugs inside on the wall and possibly in that dark smelly hole, too! I even had to aim at the bugs, but at that age, I did not worry about girl or boy locust—just locust.

Moving on, we come to Death Valley. Our car was full of all kinds of stuff, because crossing the desert you could not rely on American Automobile Association (AAA) at that time—you had to carry extra water. We had water bags strapped to the fenders, but I don't know if the water was for us or if the car was overheating—I guess it was probably for either purpose.

On one of our trips, my father wanted to go to Old Faithful in Yellowstone National Park. As we were getting close to the main gate, the snow became deeper. Then we met a moose in the road that started to run away from us. My father followed the moose until it found a low spot in the embankment and ran behind a very large tree. Father said he figured the poor fellow was hiding, thinking that if he could not see us, we must not be able to see him. However, the unfortunate animal had lots of antlers hanging out from behind the tree, which were quite visible. Yellowstone was closed, but I was able to go see it in later travels.

When we lived in Portland, Oregon, the landlord raised chickens. One day his wife decided to slaughter a few. As you may know, when you cut off the head of a chicken, it will run around for a while. It left a memorable impression on my young mind. Unfortunately, the landlady did this just after my mother had hung out her nice clean sheets. Need I say more? It's a pretty gory visual that I still remember to this day. Red-spotted sheets and headless chickens running around them. I do know that the landlord was very apologetic and made some kind of restitution.

I also remember a very large family, who built a bonfire to heat a washtub of water to cook spaghetti on a beach in Washington. They had a smaller pot going for sauce. It was the largest spaghetti dinner I have ever seen. Down the beach from this huge banquet was a dead whale wafting an unpleasant odor toward the Italian feast. It was a sensory event I still remember.

My father loved to fish, so I don't know why I never picked up this desire to stand or sit by a body of water and play head games with a fish. Even though I love the water and feel the desire to be by, in, or near it, that goes back to the beginning of time and the womb from which we all came.

I remember a game warden giving my father a ticket for not having a fishing license, when we thought we were in the middle of nowhere. On another day, I succeeded in luring a fawn into the back seat of our car. My father said he must have been the pet of one of the lumbermen, so I could not keep him, no matter how cute or friendly he was.

Another place we lived in was government housing and it left a lot to be desired. The walls were so thin, they seemed to amplify the neighbor's passing of gas or solids.

I am sure this why as an adult, I wanted to live in a freestanding house—at least one hundred feet away from my neighbor's. These recollections are of the northwest, but I also remember a house that my parents bought in San Diego, California. It was a nice little bungalow with an orange grove in the back. I am not sure why they bought it or why they sold it. I do know they paid $5,000 for it and I cannot imagine what it would be worth now if it is still there. As I go through life, I have gone back to where I remember having lived, but almost all these places are not as I recall them. Again, it's like my grandparents' house in Waltham, Massachusetts.

COMING HOME - MY FATHER'S LEAVE

I have always thought leave was a funny name for a vacation, but I guess in the service you must have permission to leave—as opposed to being AWOL (absent without leave). Civilians call it a vacation, but the Europeans say they are going on holiday.

The last time we came back from the West Coast, we were driving along Route 2, aka, the Mohawk Trail. On a hilly part, I looked down into a deep ravine. They say, "When your time is up, your life will flash before your eyes." I think this will be one of those flashes. I saw the most magnificent owl flying down into that forest. I have always been a photographer, so there are many pictures I would have loved to capture—this is one. However, it is only in my memory. I envy people whose profession is natural photography. This is one of the reasons I like to watch the *CBS Sunday Morning* moment of nature—even as short as it has become.

After we returned home, my parents and I went shopping in the Gilchrist's Department Store in Waltham, Massachusetts. I decided to go exploring, but after ten minutes, I realized my parents were nowhere around—at least that's how I felt. I was lost in this big store, not knowing my parents were watching me. They followed me, as I went off on one of my first adventures. Then, after complete panic had set in, they came to my rescue. In their own way, without any scolding, they taught me not to wander off.

This was also the store that I remember visiting the Easter Bunny. It was a big rabbit and I could see human eyes inside this large bunny's head. That strange memory has stayed with me all these years. This store also had a Christmas parade like Macy's Parade in New York City. I got a little plastic Santa Claus on a string attached to a stick. This little plastic Santa with a white fuzzy belt is still part of my Christmas every year to this day, so it is a tradition that goes back sixty-five years.

Another recollection I have happened after returning to the East Coast. When I was driving into Boston, the only tall building when looking down on the city from Route 2 was the Custom House Tower. The first skyscraper was added to the original Custom House built from 1837 to 1847 and was constructed from 1913 to 1915. 1913 was the year my father was born. The first modern skyscraper to be built was the Prudential Building, followed by the John Hancock Building.

Having lived on the West Coast, I never saw snow, other than in the mountains. When I go to visit my deceased relatives in Mt. Fieke Cemetery, I drive by an intersection that has changed very little in over sixty-five years. It is one of my first recollections of snow piled up in a city.

I realize this is of no importance to anybody else, but this is one of the few memories that has not changed in my life, so I must mention it. After my grandparents' place was gone, we stayed with my aunt and uncle on Boynton Street in Waltham, Massachusetts. Another aunt and uncle lived in Newton, Massachusetts, across town. One day, I went to visit them. I guess I did not learn my lesson in Gilchrist, because I am told that all I had on was my cowboy hat. I was found by one of my mother's friends and brought back to Boynton Street.

CHAPTER 3

Early East Coast

After the war was over, my father was stationed up and down the East Coast. At first, we would stay in apartments near the base. For some reason he was transferred a lot and moving became very hard—packing, shipping, and unpacking everything every half-year or so. My father came up with a simple solution—buy a trailer, aka a mobile home and just haul it up and down the coast wherever he was stationed.

The first trailer was six feet wide and twenty-seven long. I thought nothing of this. The refrigerator broke, so they went out to buy a new one. They came back with a new trailer, seven feet wide by thirty-six feet long. This to me was palatial. I do not think my mother thought so, because later when I got married, my wife told me that my mother had taken her aside and told her not to let me talk her into living in a trailer.

My mother was very tolerant with me. One of my really great Christmas presents was an American Flyer train. As the years passed, my Christmas present always had more train pieces added to it. I was allowed to set up every Saturday and take down Sunday evening. As the years went by, I had so much track that my plastic village was in the living room and the track went down one side of the aisle, turned under my parents bed in the back bedroom and came back up the other side. We did not have a dining room, so the table folded up and stood to one side of the living room. When the train was set up, the table and chairs had to straddle the village and tracks.

You can see why I now look at my mother as a saint. She had to put up with *me*, as my father sailed the seven seas.

When my father was home, he used to bring me to the base pool to try to teach me to swim. He told me that I used to scream that he was trying to drown me at the pool in New London, Connecticut.

I remember that it had a fuselage of a fighter plane at the deep end of the pool. This was set up to slide down and flip upside down on a ramp to teach the pilots how to escape from a downed plane.

This base also had a 100-foot dive tower. This was to learn how to escape from a submarine. I think this was built right after the submarine USS Squalus made a test dive and sunk off Portsmouth, New Hampshire.

My father never could win over my trust, as hard as he tried. But when he was at sea, my mother would bring me to a base pool and sit and read a book, while I splashed everyone within five feet of me.

I started swimming along the shallow end on the bottom and eventually as I learned to relax, I started coming to the surface, but splashing.

One hot summer, I met a boy who had a pool in his yard. His parents charged a quarter a kid on a hot day. The pool was about ten feet wide by ten feet long. I cannot remember how many kids fit into this bathtub/pool. But I think it was probably as many as twelve to fifteen. I thought nothing strange about this arrangement then, but looking back, it was one of the stranger experiences of my childhood.

I am sure this pool was in Charleston, South Carolina. This was around 1953 and I was eleven years old. It was one of the hottest summers on record for Charleston and it left a memorable impression on me about the South. Every day it never dropped below 100 degrees day or night for two weeks. If air conditioners were around then, we sure didn't have one. Living in a trailer in that heat was like being baked in an oven. Only now can I go back to this lovely city and enjoy it.

One of the problems with Charleston back then was that they were still fighting the Civil War. Me being a Yankee was not a good thing. I still tell people today that I am alive, because I could outrun some of those little rebels. What aggravated the problem was one of my friends was black. I return to Charleston every couple of years now and wonder if my black friend is still around. I can't remember his name, so I have no way of knowing.

I spent a short time in Green Cove Springs, Florida, and all I can remember here was looking down on a body of water. Only recently I learned this is the St. John's River, one of the few rivers in the United States that flows from south to north, starting from the city of Sanford and entering the Atlantic Ocean at Jacksonville.

As we traveled up and down the East Coast, my mother was aware that each school system marched to a different drummer and I was never in sync with the next school. She would call ahead to learn where they were in each subject and then she would try to tutor me in what the new system was doing. Math was always the biggest problem. I always seemed to be behind. Sometimes they were on fractions, which I would know nothing about and other times it was multiplication or division. Looking back on this problem of always being out of sync with my new school system, I can see that not being the brightest star in the universe was not entirely my fault.

When the war was over and my father came home on leave, we would visit my great-aunt and my great-grandmother in Massachusetts. I never really thought about my father's parents—they just were not there and he never talked about them. It wasn't until many years later that I learned of his sad family history. My great-aunt really had acted as my father's mother even though she was only 13 or 14 years older than him. She lived in one of the few structures still standing from my childhood and only about six miles from where I lived in Tewksbury for forty years.

When I was very young, there was a small garage filled with the heirlooms of my great-grandparents. While my father was away, my great aunt decided that all the antiques and history of the family and his law business should be given to Good Will. I know this hurt my father dearly, but he just shook his head, because like everything else that had happened, it was done and there was nothing he could do about it.

The other thing I remember about this house was that it had not been modernized and it had a chemical toilet off the kitchen. This was simply a bucket with lime in a toilet-shaped container. When this was full, it would be brought out to the outhouse on the far side of the garage and dumped. On good days there would just be a trip to the outhouse and at night, there was the bed pan, aka "Thunder Jug," under my great-aunt's bed. Whenever we were there visiting, I slept in her bedroom, so when she had to go, she would tell me to look away.

In the winter, there was no central heat. The house was heated by a small kerosene heater in the parlor and by an old, very ornate cast iron coal stove in the kitchen. With this type of heating the rooms, the upstairs would go down into the twenties on very cold nights.

In the summer, we would go camping in either the White Mountains in New Hampshire or Baxter State Park in Maine. My parents slept in an umbrella tent and I slept next to theirs. One night my mother wakes my father up and said that something was scratching on the tent. My father said, "Go back to sleep, you're imagining things. The next day a guy that had been sleeping in a station wagon next to us told my father of a bear that came through the camp, stopped at our tents, then proceeded to walk over to his cooler, open it, and ate all his steaks and bacon. This was in Baxter State Park. At this park we went for a hike and came across a moose print still filling with water in a marshy area.

Leaving this campground and driving into Great Northern Paper Company's property, we come across a sign that simply said: "This is God's country—let's not make it look like hell." Simply stated instead of: "No Fires."

Most of our camping trips were in the White Mountains in New Hampshire. We went there almost every summer in the same two weeks. There were the same people camping in the same campsites. One year when we get there, one of the other campers had a brand new tent and my father went over to admire it.

The fellow told my father he had to buy a new one, because one day returning from the store as drove into the camp, he saw a bobcat enter his tent. He figured he would just wait until the cat tired of his exploring and left. As he sat there another bobcat thought it was also a great place to explore. The fight that ensued shredded his old tent.

Another impressive thing I remember about our times in the

woods happened in the early to mid-fifties. As we walked through the woods in the White Mountains, he pointed out trees laying on the ground and starting to rot. He said, "See these trees. These were felled by the hurricane of 1938. I do not think a hurricane has felled trees that far north since."

Where I lived in Portsmouth, Rhode Island, the old timers talked of how bad it had been on the coast. They get hit more often, but in New England a storm of that strength that far inland is rare. One of my neighbors has a book that shows the fury of the '38 storm. The book shows a 450-foot freighter setting in a backyard in Fall River, Massachusetts, a good twelve miles from the sea. It had blown up through Narragansett and Mount Hope Bay in Rhode Island.

The first place my father was stationed on the East Coast was Norfolk, Virginia. Going there, we took the ferry across the Chesapeake that now has the Bay Bridge tunnel. We landed near Virginia Beach and this is my first recollection of Spanish moss. We got an apartment and I found several baby mice. I thought they were cute and brought them home to be my pets. My mother did not like that idea and I had to get rid of them. I cannot recall how that was done, but I do know I did not have them for long.

Whenever my father was stationed at another port, instead of packing and unpacking, they went out and bought a trailer to go from port to port. And when he got transferred he just hooked up the trailer and off we would go. The problem then was that there were no interstates and we would have to go through cities large and small and along back roads.

Once when my father stopped to get gas, he was talking to a truck driver, asking directions on how to get to Norfolk. The truck driver gave him the information and then told my father to just follow him and we would meet at the Red Apple Restaurant. We followed him for some time and all was well, until we came to a funeral procession. The truck driver just floored it and flew past them. However, my father's 1950 six-cylinder Chevy with an automatic transmission just did not have the power to follow the truck. An hour later, my father finds the Red Apple diner and the truck driver is coming out the door laughing. I do not think my father thought this was that funny.

Another time when he didn't see the humor in the moment, he was pulling the trailer through New York City and I had to pee. He gave me a bottle and said to go in this. As I am feeling better after I fill the bottle, I notice that we had gone through the same intersection three times. I point this out and from what he said, I think he was already aware of this. He was a very mild-mannered person, but I did have a way of trying his patience sometimes.

When we lived in Norfolk for a second time, a circus came to town. I lived right in back of the field where they were setting up the big top and they gave tickets to anyone who helped them. I could not have been any older than twelve and I cannot remember how I helped. I think I held stakes as someone drove them in. In any case, I got a ticket to the show for my labors, as insignificant as they were.

That same field was a cornfield and I remember running through it, but tripping and driving a cornstalk into my shin. My father was off at sea, so when I came home, my mother had to dig out the cornstalk. Well, she didn't get it all and the shin became infected. The next day I go to school and there was a demon girl who took pleasure out of kicking boys in the shin with her metal-tipped shoes. It was just my luck she decided to pick my infected shin to kick. I will not go into the details of how I reacted, but I know it is the only time I ever did any harm to the opposite sex.

After staying after school, I had to go home and explain to my mother what had happened. Meanwhile she had to figure out what to do about my inflamed shin—walk-in clinics were not around then. I do not think we had any medical insurance that covered cornstalks in inflamed shins, so she lays me down on the bed and gave me a damp face cloth to clinch in my teeth. I am not sure if this was to muffle the screaming or help lessen the pain, as she pins me down and squeezes the inflamed hole as hard as she can. Apparently because of the puss in the wound, the remaining piece of cornstalk came shooting out like the man that came out of the cannon at the circus. For many years there was a scar on my leg and the pain lodged in the dark recesses of my brain cells, but the pain has faded to a distant memory.

Shortly after this incident, Hurricane Carol came calling. It was 1954 and it had rained many days before the winds came. So the huge tree that hung over our little trailer was starting to lean. Seeing that my father was at sea, the owner of the park came down and unblocked the trailer. Then he pulled it out of harm's way of the falling tree. I think he had to go around the park and do this several times.

Meanwhile being the child that I was, I take my bike to the end of the street pushing it against the wind and rain. When I get to the other end of the street, I hop on my bike and probably hit forty mph before being blown back down the street with the 70 to 80 mph winds. I have admitted I was not the brightest star in the universe when I was a kid. (Some say I have not changed as adult.)

Up to 1955 I had lived in the south more than the north and sounded more like a Rebel than a Yankee. This does not mean much to the people in the north, because the war was not in their backyard. I am sure things have changed, because so many people having moved south from New England. But in my travels in the South today, I still see the Confederate flag flying off pickup trucks in the deep and not so deep South. Only recently one was raised on a flag pole on a closed Perkins restaurant. As you can tell there is still a scar in my brain cells from having lived in the south as a child. Tom Lehrer has an excellent song about this called *Dixie Pixie*. I will say no more on this subject.

From here on I have lived in the north and only traveled south for vacations and retirement. I do have a parting shot on this subject. The movie, *Deliverance,* really said it all. Now I am done.

CHAPTER 4

Early Rhode Island

Moving to Quonset Point or technically North Kingston, Rhode Island, was great. If I had money (like I do not have money), this area is where I could retire to or at least have a second home. I moved my boat down here for a couple of years to Portsmouth, Rhode Island, In doing so, what should have taken me one-and-a-half hours took three to four hours to go through and around Boston. I ended up in Danvers at the Danversport Yacht Club and kind of back to Salem Harbor, where Jack and I started out. I had a conversation with one of the fellows in the marina. He said he was getting ready to retire in a couple of years and did not know where to go. He asks, "Where would you go?"

I said, "I'd be right here in Rhode Island."

The winters are mild and the summers are cooled by the ocean breezes. This is why little Rhode Island is where I could retire. The smallest state with the largest name, "Providence Plantation of Rhode Island," is where I would hang my hat. What is strange is as I am writing this chapter, I am retired in Bokeelia, Florida.

Having lived in Portsmouth, Rhode Island, for four years while in high school, we only had one snowstorm. Snow is so infrequent there that they did not have a plow and they had to clear the road with a road grader.

Now you are probably wondering why I went to Bokeelia, Florida, when I speak so highly of Rhode Island. I go back to my statement of, "If I had money, like I do not have money." I will talk about Pine Island, Florida, at the end of the book.

Except for the area around Providence, which is now the capital of Rhode Island, the state is not very populated. Newport use to be the capital, but it was very vulnerable to attacks from the British. When I lived in Rhode Island and they were remodeling homes in Newport, they were still finding cannon balls lodged in the walls of the old Newport houses and divers were finding cannon balls in Newport Harbor.

It was in North Kingston where I built my first boat—it was small, flat-bottomed, and would not float. That reminds me of another great book by Farley Moet, *The Boat Who Wouldn't Float.* I built my boat out of green lumber. My father always thought it was better to learn by experience than by being told. This means that after the boat was screwed together, the green wood dried up and I had a quarter of an inch gap between each board. Now I have to get caulking and, yes, a lot of it to fill the gaps and sink the boat, so the wood would swell. After time, my little craft was swamp worthy. It never really saw the high seas—I stuck to water two feet or less. Nevertheless, my boating days had begun.

Apparently my father felt sorry for me with my first endeavor. He went out and bought the plans for a plywood boat, which he pretty much built himself. He would let me hold something sometimes just so I could say that I helped. But he kept me away from the real technical stuff after seeing my first attempt. This is parked next to a canal at my double-wide in St. James City, Florida.

God only knows where the rotting pieces of my first boat are. I know it was used as a platform to keep my father's locker off the ground for some time.

Another significant time I remember is going on the base at Quonset Point with him and being in a hangar where he worked. He would say, "See that plane? It is worth a million dollars." That's the first time I realized the government could really spend money.

Quonset Point is the home of the Sea Bees and part of the navy. It is the workhorse of the Navy now, but especially during World War II building ports, bridges, and yes—Quonset huts and runways. A lot of people do not know this, but these simple little half-can structures that are all over the world came out of this base and are named after it. I actually helped disassemble one and as simple as they were, they were they were really rugged. This hut was on Beaver Tail on Jamestown Island. That night we chose to sleep on the fog horn tower instead of in the Quonset hut. This seemed like a pretty cool idea, until the fog horn started to blast at four o'clock in the morning. You are probably wondering why we were disassembling a Quonset hut. It was simple—it had been donated to our Boy Scout Explorer Troop as a club house. This is also a confession. We were not supposed to be on the tower, but it sounded like a great idea at the time.

I had a pretty close group of friends in North Kingston, but there was a kid who wanted to be initiated into our group. Across the street was a sandpit and in the middle was an Indian grave site. How we got him to climb up this mound without knowing what was going on, I cannot remember. I do know we had him blindfolded and it was dusk when we got to the top. We told him to count to ten and we all jumped off the top of the mound. Then we left him with the graves as it got dark. It was not a very good thing to do, but he survived and we accepted him into our group.

Close to where I lived, there was a swimming hole with a deep blue spring in the middle of it. At the end of the school year, it was really hot and we were on half-day sessions. I went in the afternoon, so every morning I went swimming for four days during this stretch of time. That's when I got the worst sunburn I have ever had in my life. They now know that when this happens when you're young, it can come back to bite you in your adult years as melanoma—then you have to have it cut out. The doctor numbed the area with a needle before he picked up his scalpel and started to cut it out. I do not know if he was in a hurry or if he really did think the area was numb—whatever the situation, it was not numb and I told him in no uncertain words that it wasn't! He seemed surprised about this and waited a whole extra couple of minutes. Finally it was numb and he cut out the infected area.

CHAPTER 5

High School Years

When we moved this time, it was to Portsmouth, Rhode Island, and it was time for me to go to high school. My father had always promised I could go to one high school, so he arranged his duty so that I could live in one spot for four years and go to Rogers High School. I lucked out, because this school was brand new and it was a great school.

How he worked this out, I do not know. As I said before, I think this is one of the best areas in the country and Rogers is one of the best schools. I guess every kid feels this way about his or her school, but my class was the first one to go through it completely. It was one of the first high schools—if not the very first—to be built on the design of a college campus. A leading magazine of the day featured the design in an article at the time when it was rated as one of the top ten schools in the country. Its sports teams were the best in the state and it was one of the only schools in New England that had a junior ROTC Program. Therefore, we were the first junior ROTC group nationally.

Portsmouth, Rhode Island, is on the north end of Aquidneck Island and Newport was on the south end, with Middletown in the center. My ride to school was on a Short Line bus. This company ran from Boston to Providence to Newport. Basically, it was the same type of bus that Greyhound used. I was in the ROTC program and one of my instructors lived in Tiverton, Rhode Island, which was further out than my bus stop.

The Short Line bus was very comfortable and nothing like a school bus. However, if my instructor passed my stop before the bus came, he would stop and pick me up, as well as any other ROTC cadets. The really unusual thing about this ride was that his hobby was restoring old Packards. I think he had two or three of these cars, which were luxury tanks.

He was also the ROTC rifle team instructor and one of the best in the country. Almost the whole elite rifle team of West Point came from our high school ROTC rifle team. One of the reasons the team was so good was that basically, we had an unlimited amount of ammunition for the team to use when practicing and a firing range in the basement of one of the shop buildings. The deep pockets for the ammunition was compliments of William Randolph Hearst of the Hearst publishing fame. I never knew how he found our rifle team or how we found him, but I toured the Hearst Castle in San Simeon, California, and learned he was a very strong advocate of our servicemen.

Most of our ROTC students went into the service with a rank higher than private. I was the supply officer in my senior year and I can remember going through an incredible amount of ammunition. Our rifle team was the best in the country. Every year, we went to fire against the freshmen West Point team and like I said, most of its members came from Rogers rifle team. The year I was a senior, they went out to West Point for a match and we lost by one point. The sad part was that one of our members shot two points below his average. He was a friend of mine and you could not talk to him for about a month after that.

Hunting on Aquidneck Island was common back then. There was a bounty on fox, because of the number of chicken farms in the area. One day my friend shot a fox and we actually had it for supper that night. This is where I learned what the expression, "it tasted gamey" meant. He also had the head mounted and put on his bedroom wall. Whenever his dog went into that room, the dog would growl at it.

One problem that arose was a bread delivery truck would leave bread on the doorstep of a small variety store. Two crows, that he named Sam and Murphy, would peck through the wrapping and ruin the bread. This was resolved by getting a small tarp to cover the bread. To this day, whenever I see two crows, I think of Sam and Murphy. There are books written about crows and ravens. They are of the same family and the story goes that if the ravens leave the Tower of London, England will fall, but I digress.

Along with ROTC, my other activity was track. As I have already mentioned, I was a pretty good runner, so I decided to try out for the track team. The coach in his ultimate wisdom sized me up for the half mile, which I enjoyed. I did not have the speed for sprints, the agility for hurdles, strength for shot put, javelin, and discus or the endurance for the mile. The half mile fit me like a glove.

My best time in my senior year was two minutes and four seconds, which was good back then. Not so good today, but that time got me the state championship for the class A half mile. Of course, we were the smallest state in the country.

A lot of people including me never think of track as a very dangerous sport. But in the two years that I was on the track team, I saw two kids almost killed and another one broke his foot. The first kid I saw at a state meet was vaulting. He landed sharply on his head, so that his neck bent to a ninety-degree angle with a snap. Somehow they were able to reset his neck and he lived. The second incident was even stranger. We had a bull of a guy who could throw the javelin as far as anybody in the whole state. One day when he was practicing, he threw that spear a huge distance. When he let it go, nobody was in his range, but to everybody's horror, a young boy ran out onto the field after he had let it go. It missed the kid by about a foot. The broken foot was caused by someone who simply laid a sixteen-pound shot put on a bench in the locker room. It rolled off onto the cement floor and landed on the foot of an athlete who was standing near the bench.

Our miler won the state championship that summer. That summer, he was swimming off one of the Newport beaches, when he cramped up and went down like a rock. He drowned right after he graduated. He should have known that running and swimming do not go together. He was not a close friend, but I really liked him.

What was sad and, I still find strange to this day, is that his brother was a half-miler with me. We almost always took first and second in the state. He never beat me though. I did not think anything about this and was thrilled we were taking first and second in all our meets. At our graduation, he signed my yearbook with: ""Too bad you had to be better than me or we could have been better friends!"

I can tell this story now, because they have both are gone now. I believe he died in Vietnam. One other footnote—a couple of years later, he had to let it be known that he even thought he would never beat me, but he got a full scholarship to college. I had never planned to go to college, because I really did not think I had the brain cells for higher education. After all, I had been bounced from pillar to post in thirteen schools systems for eight years, before finally being able to spend the next four great years at one high school.

One day I remember sitting in algebra class and from the window I could see the ocean. My father was going to sea for six months heading for Europe. I did not learn much that day as I sat there and watched his ship sail over the horizon. Another time while I sat there, a freighter had gone on the rocks and it took a couple of weeks to break up and sink. I found this very distracting, loving the sea and boats even back then.

As the years passed, I would frequently go back to my new ultra-modem school and painfully watch it age until one day, I almost felt like not going back any more. Everything has to age, but when I finally returned—lo and behold, it had been rehabilitated and almost looked better than new! I can't remember how long ago this was, but when I went online, I saw that they were talking about building another new school to the tune of 153.33 million dollars. There was also a proposal to redo the old school for 103 million dollars. I guess there is quite a fight about all of this. I find this crazy, because when I went there, they had built this massive college campus for three million dollars. I guess I am really dating myself. However, this is my alma mater, because I do not have a college to think of in this way.

Going to this school was a strange experience for me in other ways, also. Because it was Newport, some of the kids that went to Rogers lived in mansions and they became my friends. It was strange to live in a trailer and call on friends who were living in mansions and, yes, even dating some of these girls. In some cases, I would have to pick them up at the servant's door, although I never thought their parents might have been the servants.

Once one of my classmate's parents went to Europe for a month's vacation. While his parents were gone, he decided to throw a party. This mansion could hold several hundred kids, which it did. Back then, kids were less destructive, but when the party was over, it still took him a couple of weeks to get the place cleaned up. He thought he was home free, but the nuns at Salve Regina College next door knew his parents, so his party was revealed. He had kept everything under control, so even the police didn't know about it. However, one guy did get taken in for trying to find out if a Volkswagen really did float, as he drove it down to the beach around the corner. (Side note—it did.)

The mansion literally had two staircases in the main hall and, as the song goes, one going up—the other just for show. At the top of the stairs was a hall with a balcony and a railing. I remember somebody walking on the railing like a tight rope. Why he did not fall is beyond me. I also remember sitting in the kitchen fireplace with four other kids. If you have ever seen the movie *High Society*, this is the road that the mansion was on and where I learned to drive.

I liked almost all my teachers, except for one. I guess I can talk about her now, because she was old in 1958. She was not that bad, but I do not think she liked me. She taught Spanish and her name was Mrs. Olsen. At that time, there was a boxer by the name of BOBO Olsen. So around the school, she was known as BOBO. Although nobody ever called her this to her face, she knew that was her nickname. One day in my ultimate wisdom, I decided I would ask her what BOBO meant in Spanish, knowing full well that it meant *fool*. Well, for that question, I got an evening of detention and was sent to the dean's office. Now, here is another person I can talk about, because if he wasn't 80 at that time, he was close to it. He was a nice man, but I can still remember his breath, even as I write this story. The poor man had the worst halitosis I have ever run across.

I go into his office and he sits me down. looks very calmly at me, and asks, "If you lived next door to a house that had a fence around it and vicious dog was in that yard, would you stick your hand in that yard?"

Well, that was a no brainer, so I said, "No!!!"

"Well," he said, "Stop harassing, Mrs. Olsen."

After five minutes of enlightenment, I still had to serve my detention. When I arrived, there were three other guys that had also stuck their hands into that fence.

We all sat there quietly and did our homework while serving our time with the *fool*. As the afternoon drew to a close and our time for release was imminent, Mrs. Olsen went to her closet and took out the rattiest beaver coat I have ever seen. One of the other fellows that was doing time, too, simply said, "Should we shoot it now or wait till it's in season?" This is one of the funniest lines I have ever heard in my life. I thought we were going to have to call the paramedics to revive her. After she composed herself, we got another half hour from the vicious dog.

I had to write a book report and I was told it could be any book about anything. Having lived in the south, I found one about Andersonville Prison. I thought I was being cute, because the book was about a quarter of an inch thick and three by five inches in size. Strangely this book is the one I remember most out of all the books I had to read in high school, with possible exception of Hemingway's *Old Man and the Sea.*

Having lived in the South and in the North and seeing both sides of history, I realize the scar on this country. More men died in the Civil War between the North and the South than in World War I and World War II put together.

The Civil War's worst villain from the South was Captain Henry Wirz, the commander of the Andersonville Prison. He was the only person out of this war who was convicted of war crimes. It's said that half of the prisoners from the Civil War died in this prison. When he was hanged on November 10, 1865, he said he was only carrying out his orders.

Major General Tecumseh Sherman was the north's worst villain, leading 60,000 soldiers from Atlanta to Savannah, Georgia, a distance of 225 miles from November 15 to December 21, 1864. His purpose was for the people of the South to see the futility of secession.

The strange thing that has stayed with me from school is the word *shebang*. Four years in years in high school and I come out with this as one of my memorable words. I know this sounds crazy—I agree. Today the word is strictly slang meaning, "the whole ball of wax" or "the whole enchilada." To northerners imprisoned in Anderson Prison in Georgia during the Civil War, it meant their survival. A shebang was a hole dug in the ground covered with anything to be found that protected them from the sun and heat in the summer and the bitter cold of the Georgia winters. I have gone back now and find this word first used by poet Walt Whitman to mean "a rustic dwelling" and later Mark Twain used it to mean "a vehicle." I know I have digressed big time on this one, but it has stayed with me all my life and I have to include it somewhere. I guess I should apologize.

Talking about apologies, I had a friend at that time who had a quirky habit. He said that if we ever went anywhere and had a really great time, we should go back there, just to apologize.

Another book report I gave was on the state of South Dakota. The computer was not around then, so I wrote to the Chamber of

Commerce of Pierre, the capital of South Dakota, and I received a pretty thick package on the many attractions of the state. This left a memorable impression in my young mind. For the rest of my life, I wanted to go see this interesting state—Mt. Rushmore, Crazy Horse, and the Badlands.

Sturgis wasn't big back then, even though it had its first rally before I was born. I will cover this part of my life in my experiences on my road trips around the country. I feel everybody, if they have the finances, health, and time, should do a road trip around the country at least once—even though I still hear about places I missed.

Another thing that has stayed in my mind is marching with the high school band as part of the ROTC unit. To this day when I watch a parade, I think back to that marching beat.

This brings to mind two great parades I have seen in New England. The Fourth of July parade in Bristol, Rhode Island, is among the biggest and best in the country. The center line in the street is actually painted red, white, and blue. Bands come from all over the country to march in this parade.

Another parade I always liked was the Bunker Hill Day Parade in Charleston, just outside of Boston. (The movie, *The Town*, was filmed there.)

My lazy summer days living in Portsmouth, Rhode Island, consisted of water skiing and swimming in the Sakonnet River. I also worked for a doctor as his handyman, cutting the grass, trimming bushes, and maintaining a dirt road to his summer camp. His main house, office, and summer camp were all a third of a mile from each other. He was off on Wednesday and he would work with me and tell me interesting stories of his medical school days and other experiences he had.

One thing he told me was that during life, things will happen to you that you know could have never happened before. This was the first time I had ever heard of *Deja vu*. Guess this has happened to everyone at one time or another. Whenever I have such a feeling, I remember this doctor who looked like a truck driver, but was a great and intelligent man. He was an anesthesiologist and often needed for emergencies. When one arose, he would call the state police and they would give him an escort. While on the way, he taped what he would need for the operation, then gave the information to a nurse while he scrubbed up.

From the time he called to the time he could be in the operating room could be less than half an hour, which was incredible in the late fifties. I look back on him as one of the most interesting people I have ever known. When we worked together around his property, he always gave me a full day's pay, even though we often took an hour for water skiing and swimming. Every once in a while, he would give me a twenty to take his daughter to Lincoln Park. Twenty dollars was a lot of money back then, when you could get a haircut for a dollar.

Another interesting person I met had been a rum runner in the days of Prohibition. He was an uncle of one of my friends and told some great stories. We went to see him one day and when we got to his home, he was welding a bicycle frame. The frame was really hot and he was holding it with his bare hands. Maybe he didn't have any feeling left in his hands after doing this kind of work for so long.

He told of how they would run in the boat on dark nights with the liquor tied onto salt blocks that would sink. When the Coast Guard would chase them, they would throw the liquor overboard and it would sink. When they were boarded, no whiskey could be found.

The next morning, they would go back and pick up the cases as they floated to the surface, the salt blocks having melted away.

He also showed us some interesting weapons from those days. He had a sixteen-gauge pistol sawed down from a sixteen-gauge shotgun, and a ten-gauge shotgun with a full chock, as well as an old blunderbuss with a bell-shaped muzzle that would fire anything that would fit down the barrel. This was fired with black powder and a flint. He asked if I would like to fire one of them. Being really leery of the black powder and the blunderbuss, I choose the ten-gauge. To this day, I remember the kick of that shotgun. I regret that I didn't choose the blunderbuss, since that chance will never come again. I could tell by the gleam in his eyes that those were his halcyon days. He was one of the most unique persons I have ever met—truly a person out of our country's history.

Pillars of the Portsmouth community were Mr. and Mrs. Webb of Cherry and Webb clothing stores. I do not think the stores were known nationally, but they were all over New England. As the story goes, like Sears he bought a truckload of women's dresses on an unclaimed truck and sold them off. With the profits, he bought another load and so on, until he started selling his goods out of a store in Fall River, Massachusetts. This is the way Sears started, only his unclaimed merchandise was watches. Sears in his brilliance started a catalog to go to the heartland of the country where people did not have access to the stores of the city. He was even selling homes and cars, Kaisers, and mopeds, but I digress.

I never met Mr. Webb, but I did know Mrs. Webb, a very pleasant and reserved lady. She drove a 1958 Cadillac Eldorado Brougham. It had a stainless steel top and a leather interior, of which only 304 were manufactured. The only other one I have seen was in a car museum in Reno, Nevada.

One day she parked it at the top of a hill going to St. Paul's Episcopal Church in Portsmouth, Rhode Island. When she came out, she found it resting unscratched between two trees at the bottom of the hill. She was proud of owning this car and she protected it carefully by driving it into her barn, which had a turntable in the corner. When the car was put on this turntable, she would press a secret squirrel switch that would turn it 90 degrees and it could not be removed.

Because of the mild weather in Portsmouth, Mr. Webb was able to import some very exotic plants, trees, and bushes. The mansion and grounds were magnificent. These two interesting people had adopted a boy and when he grew up, he married a friend of my sister. Portsmouth, Rhode Island, was a small town and everybody knew everybody. Even though I was blow-in navy brat, I still felt liked I belonged there.

When Mrs. Webb died, I went with my friend to help close out the estate. I had never at that time been in a more elegant private home with the exception of the mansions in Newport. I found it fascinating that people actually lived like that—seen through the eyes of a boy who grew up in a trailer. Each piece of art had a little light over it. Mrs. Webb went around and turned each one on in the morning and off at night. Up in the attic, which was a full third story, were box after box of her purchases that had never been used or opened, with the receipts for each bag or box still with each.

Years later I returned to this grand old mansion after it had been turned into a restaurant. The barn was gone, but some of the exotic flora was still thriving on the perimeter of the property. Yes, the turntable was still there, but a mystery to the owner of the restaurant.

I told my waitress the story of this turntable and she went to the owner and cleared up the mystery.

As the years passed, the last time I drove by the property, it had been remodeled as condos. Time marches on.

The father of one of my friends was a very quiet man, who had a way of looking right through you. My friend said he had been on the deepest surviving submarine dive of World War II, which had been under attack by Japanese depth charges for several days. They finally blew debris out of the torpedo tubes to make it look like the submarine had blown up. At that time, that depth was still classified and top secret.

Another night—it was kind of spontaneous—as we were driving past the state police barrack, one of the guys decided to yell out some uncomplimentary comments. Well, it was a warm night and they had their windows open. We were riding in back of a pickup truck and they heard every word. The police were out of the barracks and had us pulled over in under two miles, even though we were doing 45 mph. They brought us back to the barracks and called all our parents, except mine. My parents did not have a phone. Nothing happened except we had to promise not to do it again.

Another time, we knew where the state police and the town cops would meet on a slow day and drag. The state police always won. Things were not as serious back then and word was the chief's philosophy was that the quicker you drove through his town, the quicker he was rid of you.

We were sailing one day and it seems we were being watched. We capsized and the town's amphibious duck, like the ones Boston has for tours, was called to rescue us. Well, the duck was not very fast and when they finally showed up, we had righted the sailboat and were about to get underway. We criticized them for taking so long, but had to give a public apology in the local newspaper.

A little side note was that the person who owned the sailboat and was in charge was the minister of our church. The other side note was the duck that had come out to rescue us had been bought in the mid-fifties and was driven back by one of the firemen in town. I believe it had been stopped by the Pennsylvania state police, because they felt there had to be something illegal about it, so they went over the duck for quite a while before they finally let him go. When he told the story to the fire chief, they both went out to the duck and looked it over. Finally, the chief said the license plate was not up to date. They both had a good laugh, because the state cop had not noticed that.

I remember hearing that Dwight Eisenhower, aka "Ike," was going to be in a parade in Newport, so I hopped on my bike and peddled in to see him. He loved to come to Newport to play golf. Of all the contemporary presidents, I think Ike was the greatest. His military genius saved us in World War II. According to two books I read about him, one book says he lost only one serviceman in his eight years in office. The other book I read said he did not lose any servicemen.

Because he saw what the autobahn did for Germany, he realized this country needed an updated highway system, aka, the Interstate Eisenhower Federal Highway. He also incorporated the St. Lawrence Seaway for the Midwest to move products from the Great Lakes. He backed up integration in the southern schools by dispatching federal troops to safely escort a group of students (soon to be known as the Little Rock Nine) to their classes in the midst of violent protests from angry white students and townspeople in September 1957 in Little

Rock, Arkansas. This was one of the most important steps for all black students in the South.

And last, but not least, he knew to stay out of the Middle East, because they have been at each other's throats for centuries. I do not understand why he does not get more recognition as one of our greatest presidents.

The other president I've seen was George Bush, Sr. I saw him in Biddeford Pool, Maine. He would come up from his Kennebunkport summer home for coffee. The security for a cup of coffee and his boat trip on Fidelity was incredible, with a sub chaser plane overhead and a destroyer offshore. One day George is motoring by an acquaintance of mine and my friend offers him a beer. George pulls over and quickly guzzles it down. Then he looks at the secret serviceman and says, "Too late."

At that time, my friend criticizes the condition of George's boat. Three weeks later, George went by my friend with a sparkling clean boat and he calls back, "Is this better?" Another reason I admire George is how the Secret Service wanted to close the cove as better security for the Bush's summer home. However, he said, "No, that is how the lobster men make their living." Again, I digress.

Back to Portsmouth, Rhode Island—at the end of Sakonnet River, there is a little enclave called Island Park, which is about a mile from where I used to live. My mother would send me there for my one haircut once a week. About the only building standing was the barber shop and it was on the other side of the road from the beach. This was all taken out in the hurricane of 1938. Today this has all been reconstructed. What fascinates me is that most of the buildings have been restored without being built on stilts.

Coming from Tiverton, Rhode Island, to Portsmouth, Rhode Island, there is a bridge that was new when I lived there. That bridge is now being replaced by another one. It's things like this that make me feel old. It is not the physical things—it's the mental stuff.

On the old bridge, when I was a kid going over it, I saw one of the strangest accidents I have ever seen. Two identical 1956 Plymouth sedans—even the same color—hit head on. When they bounced back apart, it looked like you were looking at a three-way mirror.

Because we moved so much, my parents' friends were from all over the country (from the service). One couple I remember my parents staying in contact with was a fellow my father was stationed with who had a twin brother in the Midwest. That man and his twin brother married twin sisters and they built their houses next to each other—they called it twin acres. How cool is that? Their children did come at different times. It was sad for the Xmas cards to diminish as the years went by.

My father did physically keep in touch with one friend. I believe his name was Matear or something that sounded like that. When this fellow retired, a friend of his who was well off set him up in business with the first VW dealership in northern New York. My parents went out to visit him several times. One time they brought me with them. He had a navy longboat off his house on Lake Erie and a big game room in his basement. I am not talking about a pool table—we are talking big game rifles and two freezer lockers full of bear, elk, and deer. His friend had a seaplane and they would fly all over North America to go hunting and fishing. His wife was an excellent cook. It's the only time I have had bear and she really knew how to cook it!

I know my father missed his navy buddies. I remember one buddy who came to visit him from California. He operated one of those port cranes that load freighters. He was an interesting character.

My father also missed being on a ship, so when he bought their house, he went into the basement and anything that did not move was painted battleship gray. When he went below—aka, to the basement, he felt at home.

While I am talking about my father, I have to say every son should respect their father and think of their father as special. But my father could do things that amazed me. When he was young, he pulled parts out of a junkyard and built his own car. He could play the harmonica. I can remember him walking on his hands. I have tried this time and again and could never do it—I do not know how he did. He was a machinist and I have read his notes and calculations. Overwhelming. I have truly digressed.

The area around Portsmouth and Tiverton, Rhode Island, and Fall River, Massachusetts, I later learn that three of my neighbors all grew up in this area. Twenty-five to thirty years later, we all talk about our childhood spent in an area ninety miles away, like we all knew each other back then. How strange is that?

One thing I remember about Tiverton was there was a fuel port at the bottom of the hill and two gas stations at the top of the hill that were having a gas war. Each tried to put the other out of business and they went as low as ten and eleven cents per gallon. This was great, because as kids we could chip in twenty-five cents apiece and go water skiing all day.

Driving through Fall River was not bad in the summer, but in the winter the mayor was a purist. He believed when it snowed, whether they had an inch or a foot, the good Lord put it there, so the good Lord taketh away.

We would almost always go to my aunt and uncle's house on the weekends. We would drive up Friday night or Saturday morning ·and come back Sunday night. I enjoyed staying there with my cousins, even though they were much younger. Staying in their house was like visiting a grand old mansion. My uncle was very talented and started remolding or should I say rehabilitating this old gem of a farm house of the Victorian era as soon as he moved in. It became a life project to bring the house back to its original grandeur. Pocket doors led to the living room and dining room. A round turret protruded from the right front corner of the house and it had a wraparound porch from the left front to the back right-hand side of the house. A pass-through went from the kitchen to a serving hutch in the dining room.

The house was out in the country and I enjoyed going off into the woods and skating on a pond behind a very old cemetery that went back to the founding of Stow, Massachusetts, on May 16, 1683. This house was even harder for me to see sold than when I had to sell my parents' home. Down in the back was a field that I used to fly the kites my uncle taught me how to make. They were better than anything that you could buy. The only limit to how high I could get them to go up was the strength of the many balls of string I tied together.

The cemetery had some interesting tombstones. Every Thanksgiving for about forty years after the meal, I would walk around and read the gravestones. I knew that the ones with weeping willows on the top died of a natural death and the ones with a skull on the top died of an unnatural death—disease, plague, or killed. The most unusual gravestone is no longer there. In my youth, I had found a stone that said something to this effect: "Here lies (next came a name that I cannot remember) beheaded by command of the King of England and the head returned to the King." I know this headstone had to be stolen, since it is no longer there. I found reading old tombstones very interesting. I know there is a book published on this very subject.

A story that comes to mind is once I worked with a fellow whose name I have to use is Fred Penny. On his tombstone he says he would like to have, "If you find yourself without money, dig six feet and find a Penny."

I have heard that W.C. Fields had, "I'd rather be in Philadelphia," on his headstone. Another one that was on a tombstone in the Stow cemetery was, "As you are, so were we. As we are, so you will be." This I find very profound.

Down in back of that field where I flew my kites was a classic old swimming hole, with the rope hanging from a tree and leeches in the water. It would not be classic without the leeches. On a hot summer day this was the best spot in my world.

My uncle grew some of the best strawberries around. This is attributed to the old saying, "The acorn does not fall far from the tree," because his father's strawberries were even better. This brings to mind how his father protected his strawberry patch. He had a birder cat that could leap almost six feet when he sneaked up on an unsuspecting bird.

Speaking of acorns, this brings to mind the story of the slowest way to commit suicide. Put a noose around your neck and tie the other end of the rope around an acorn. I am sorry—I had to tell it.

My uncle's house was on Route 62, which was a very busy road. After a while, this little roadside strawberry stand became loved by all those who traveled that little part of the world. The proceeds I understand paid their taxes.

After my uncle had passed, my aunt was having a very hard time with such a large house. It was time to find a place that could take care of her. One day a fellow was driving by and saw a bolt of lightning hit the turret of her house. He ran up and rang her bell and told her to call the fire department. The station was very close and they got there quickly and put out the fire. The turret was repaired and the house was put up for sale and sold.

They brought my aunt down to a nursing home close to her daughter's home. My cousin asked if there was anything in the house that I would like.

I said, "If nobody wanted the dining room chandelier, I would give them mine to replace it and take that one." I loved that chandelier, but when I sold my house in Tewksbury, I gave it back to my cousin. It just would not fit into my Florida home.

Before I left Rhode Island, I attended Newport's first Folk Festival and got autographs from the original Kingston Trio. I still treasure them.

CHAPTER 6

Early Employment

I head north to begin my adult years.

We moved the trailer to Littleton, Massachusetts. Finding a trailer park or available lots in this area was hard. But looking back on this problem, I guess a park was in this area, because Fort Devens was very close. This was another government installation where enlisted men could move their trailers.

When my father retired from the navy, he was employed by High Voltage Engineering in Burlington, Massachusetts. My mother worked in Microwave, also in Burlington. The two companies were less than a mile apart, so as long as they worked, they were able to ride together. I got a job at Demoulas Markets. We all ended up driving some distance. After a few months, my parents find a house in Wilmington, Massachusetts. This was my father's hometown and much closer for all of us.

I stayed in this house before we actually moved in. For some reason, one night I wake up almost overcome by the fumes from the refinishing of my bedroom floor. Somehow I made it to a window and opened it for a breath of fresh air—I do not think I could have made it to the door. I went back to Littleton and waited for the fumes to dissipate.

I met three great guys working in the Wilmington Demoulas and

I wish I had stayed in touch with them. They were characters and we did almost everything together. John, Dick, and Bob—how is that for everyday names?

John was going to the New England School of Art and I would go into Boston sometimes to go to the Boston parties. I had never really experienced city life or its parties, but it was fun.

A club called the Unicorn celebrated its opening on Boylston Street with a party upstairs on the third floor. As a promotion, they had gotten a small Shetland pony to have on the sidewalk with a cone strapped on its head. It seems somebody thought it would be cute to lure this pony, aka Unicorn, up to our party. Everybody was having a great time till the police dropped by and said we had to return the pony. No charges were filled, but it was not as easy getting the pony back down the stairs as it had been going up. They say what goes up must come down, but sometimes not as easily.

John did not have a car, so I was invited everywhere he wanted to go. Along with Boston, there were art school parties on Cape Cod. It was a great day. Riding home, I had three people in the front seat and four in the back. One was a girl who thought it was fun leaning out of the back of my convertible with the top down and the sound of my cool Lakes plugs bypassing the exhaust system and growling at the nice state cop who had been following us. I say "nice state cop," because the whole thing must have seemed pretty funny to him. An overloaded car, a couple of drunk people in the back seat, rumbling Lakes plugs, and a barefoot driver doing a little more than the speed limit. It does pay to say yes sir and no sir to these figures of authority who simply handled this situation by asking me—not telling me—to close the plugs, put up the top, and go straight home doing the speed limit.

When you are young, you do strange things. Johnny and I thought it would be cool to go to New York City for a cup of coffee. When we arrived that afternoon, we spent it just walking around and looking up like most tourists do. All of a sudden, the streets were filled with thousands of people getting out of work, so we ducked into a coffee house—at least that's what we thought it was. It seems it was a pretty fancy restaurant and Johnny and I probably had ten dollars between us and neither one of us had a credit card.

We each ordered a cup of coffee and while we were sitting there nursing our coffees, the maître d' watched us suspiciously. When the couple next to us was leaving, they put a fifty dollar bill on the table to pay for their meal and the tip. This was big money to Johnny and me at this time. Johnny looked at me and then at the maître d' who was standing at the door. I could see what Johnny was thinking, so I said, "No way!"

As we were headed out of the city, we came to a stoplight. While we were sitting there, a homeless man comes up to Johnny. Seeing him smoking a cigarette, he asks for one. As the light turns green, Johnny says, "Sorry, man, this is my last one."

The homeless guy just yells as I am pulling away, "Well, throw it to me."

One time I was driving home, which was close to Johnny's house, when we passed this really attractive girl. I made some comment about how cute she was. When we reached his house, we went in and were sitting in his kitchen. Suddenly that same cute girl came walking in! That's how I met Johnny's sister for the first time.

Johnny liked to fool around, so one day he was throwing bloated cans against the wall of the garbage bin, watching them explode. Mike Demoulas came up behind him and said, "Come with me."

It was a hot day with a load of potatoes just showing up in a tractor trailer truck. Mike tells Johnny to go get enough skids to pile on the potatoes. Mike takes off his suit coat and climbs up into to the trailer. Then he proceeds to throw fifty-pound bags onto that trailer for Johnny to stack up on the skids. Mike was so mad that he had actually worked harder throwing the bags than Johnny did catching them.

Mike was a hardworking man, and one day he came up to me while I was on a coffee break and just started talking to me. In this conversation, he told me that someday he would like to have twenty stores, but at this time, he only had three. I think before he died, he had at least fifty—now I believe the count is over sixty.

The next guy in our foursome was Dick. We hung around a lot until he finally got drafted. Just before he went into the service, we decided to go to Nova Scotia, so we loaded up the Chevy and took off.

Because the car was a convertible, we wanted to put everything in the trunk. I have always had a pretty good ability to pack, but I am not going to list the entire inventory of what was in that trunk. Let's just say it was everything needed to exist for an entire week of camping—tent, food, emergency fuel, and a stove, among other things. The only thing that did not fit was one can of Dinty Moore's beef stew. Along with all of this, we had some milk in the cooler. However, when we got to the Canadian border, the Border Patrol said we could not bring the milk into their country, so we had to dump it out. We asked if we could drink it there and they said yes, so they waited while Dick and I drank our half-gallon of milk.

The car was so loaded down that if I drove at night, my headlights lit up the treetops instead of the road. The Canadian mounted police (by the way, they were mounted on brand new Bonneville Pontiacs) seeing this loaded vehicle actually stopped us to see what we were smuggling into their country. When I opened the trunk, the Mountie just shook his head and told us we could go.

Dick and I had a great time on this trip, which was the first time out of the United States for both of us. One night before going to sleep, we listened to the eerily mournful sounds of bagpipes being played down the coast. I didn't know that the next time I would hear this sound would be at my father's military funeral years later.

That was the morning we wake up to a bunch of cows around our tent. It seems the farmer was just using his cow pasture as a camp ground.

At another camp ground we thought it would be interesting to pitch our tent in front of the ladies outhouse. That way, we could say good morning to all the ladies who came and went.

On this trip, I had instructions from my uncle to drop in on his old homestead where he was born. He also wanted to be sure we would visit John Caldwell, who lived across the street from his house. I found the town and stopped to ask a lady walking down the road if she knew John. She said yes, but it was apparent that she wanted to know who I was and why I was looking for John. After we took care of all her questions, she said John was retired now, but had never done much of anything anyhow. She finally gives me the directions and we find John's house with chickens flying in and out of the windows and a goat standing at the kitchen door.

John's older brother and his wife come out of the house to greet us. They wanted to know who I was, so I explained that I was Aunt Emma and Uncle Murray's nephew. He also asked me to take a picture for my uncle. John's wife said, "Wait a minute. I have to go change." This made sense to me. seeing that her cotton dress had a three-corner tear on her left breast covered only by her bra. After a few minutes, she returned with the same dress on.

Seeing the puzzled look on my face, she said that she had to put on her boots, because she had been wearing John's. While I was there, we talked about the tidal bore that rolls up into the Bay of Fundy. They say that the tidal bore rolls in on a two-foot wave and the water rises so fast a child cannot outrun it. It's the highest in the world, reaching in excess of thirty feet.

That was the end of this trip, but regrettably I missed Oak Island. Years later, a boss put me on to following what now runs on the History Channel as *The Curse of Oak Island,* which is filmed not far from where we were.

Several years later, I returned to Nova Scotia with my wife and cousin. We were able to get to what felt like the end of North America and the world—Meat Cove—a trip back in time. I have not been able to see Canada like I have seen the United States. I would like to do the transcontinental railway like a friend of my father's raved about.

One strange event occurred in Nova Scotia was when we were getting gas. A woman pumping gas next to us was very excited as she told the attendant pumping her gas, "Our cabin's coming today." We really did not think much about this exuberant statement until we got back on the road. A few miles later, we come around the corner and meet a cabin taking up almost all of the road. Coming at us was the same very excited lady who was waiting for it.

Dick and I were up in Laconia, New Hampshire, and spotted a sign that advertised seaplane rides out of Paugus Bay off Lake Winnipesaukee. He asked if I had ever been up in a plane and I said, "No."

He said, "Let's take a ride," and I agreed. The pilot said he would take us up as soon as he pumped the water out of his pontoons to get the plane off the water. When we get into the plane and are taxiing out to take off, our wing tips are dipping into the water from the wakes of the boats around us. We finally lift off and are heading for a church steeple in downtown Laconia. He banks away from the steeple just before he almost hits it. He looked at us with a smile and says, "I do that just to make the parishioners nervous."

I said, "Not to mention, your passengers."

One day I asked Dick if he had ever been in Boston's Museum of Science and its planetarium. He said, "No," and just like our seaplane ride in New Hampshire, we are off on another adventure.

I have always been fascinated with the solar system and its many mysteries. The planetarium is where you can watch events of the solar system as they are explained to you by a narrator. One such celestial event we were going to witness was the passing of the north star from the northern latitude to dipping below the horizon. As we are sitting there, Dick realizes that this event is going to happen behind the massive celestial projector. Not realizing the acoustics in the planetarium were unbelievable, he simply leans over to me and whispers (or at least he thought he was whispering), "We are going to get screwed," meaning we were going to miss the north star dropping below the horizon. The entire audience starts laughing.

There were so many enjoyable times with my three friends. When

Dick went to boot camp, I drove him down to New York. While down there, we had a little going-away party at the Peppermint Lounge, when it was all the rage.

I really do not have many stories about Bob, except that he had a really nice Ford convertible. One day a hurricane was coming and the store we worked in had a bank being built next door. The roof was on it and the sides were the buildings on either side, but the front and back had not been closed in. So Bob drove his car into the bank to protect anything from being blown into the convertible top.

He told the story of working on his engine and taking off the valve covers of his five-year-old car. It had never been worked on since he bought it new. Laying in the pan was a well-oiled wrench.

One time when the four of us were getting together after work, we were sitting out in front of the store. All of a sudden, we were surrounded by four police cruisers. It seems the bank next to ours— Bob's protection from the hurricane earlier—had just been robbed. The police thought it was us. I guess they let us go, because none of us had any money. We told the police that if we had robbed the bank, we would not be sitting there waiting for them to come pick us up.

Another experience we had with the local law enforcement was when the store decided to try stocking at night, instead of while the store was open during the day. The police would come around and check on us. At least, this is what we thought they were doing. But it seems they were just getting friendly with us, so they could talk us into getting them some cigarettes. Well, a pack of cigarettes did not fit under the door very well, so they said to open a pack and roll each cigarette under the door separately. I do not know how long this went on, because I changed stores shortly after that.

The next store I worked in, I received a promotion—if you want to call it that. I became the dairy and frozen food manager of Demoulas' smallest store. The Demoulas were very good about giving needy people a job and one of the fellows had a heart of gold, but God had not been as kind to him in the brain department. He was as strong as a bull and when the sides of beef weighing 250 pounds each came in on hooks, he would unload the truck like nothing at all. One day he was sick and I was the only healthy one there that could unload the truck. I got it done, but I still do not know how. The sad thing about this guy was that his mother was a beast and she was always there to take his money on pay day. Sometimes she would move on him and not tell him where she went.

There was an old Greek woman who came in a couple of times a week. Somebody said that she owned quite a lot of property around the city of Lowell, Massachusetts. One day I am stocking the dairy case and she is standing to my left. I happen to look to my right and see her in the mirror putting hot dogs into her shirt. I go to inform the manager of the store, so he and a woman from the office confront her. She starts wailing about how poor she is, so they did not press charges, but told her she was not allowed in the store again. The manager was a mousy bundle of nerves without a spine.

One day Mike Demoulas comes in and with the manager comes over to me and says, "Paul, I would like you to change the frozen food case and make it more organized. I will be back in about a week and check it." He did not tell me what he wanted, so I think he just trusted my ability. You probably would not think about this, but when you rearrange an entire frozen food case, it is not an easy job. Stuff is frozen together and your hands basically stay numb for the entire time, even if you're wearing gloves.

After three days of almost losing my fingers to frostbite—strange thing to have happen in the summer—the store manager comes over to see the change. He looks at it and says it looks good, but he did not think that is what Mike had in mind, so he proceeds to tell me how I should have done it. Who am I to challenge the manager, so another three days later, I have done it the way the store manager wanted it. A short time after that, Mike comes back with the store manager and looks the case all over. He then says, "Paul, it looks very neat, but I was thinking that it should be different." He then proceeds to tell me to put it back exactly the way I had it *before* I was told to change it. Mike left and I turned around and look at the store manager and said, "Well, you can change it back, because I do not work here anymore."

I look back on that day as another big change in my life.

I have had good bosses and bad bosses, like almost everybody else and in most cases, I had been able to outlast the bad ones and enjoy the good ones. I will not talk much about the bad ones. In most cases, they were either too dumb or power-hungry to keep the job they had and they almost always did themselves in. I will say this though, my good bosses were almost always Irish. As Paul Harvey would have said, the rest of this story was about a month later, when I run into Mike and he asked me why I had left.

I told him about the store manager making me change the case to the way he wanted, but I had had it exactly the way Mike wanted it. He said he would give me a raise and put me in another store then or whenever I wanted to come back. I always respected Mike and considered him one of the best people I ever knew.

CHAPTER 7

New Hampshire and UFOs

This was about the time in my life when my parents bought some land in a little town called Gilmanton Iron Works, aka Peyton Place of Grace Metalious fame. It was on a small pond called Sawyer Lake. When we first started going up, it was pretty wild—moose, beer, and loons. There is very little in the wild more haunting than the cry of a loon at night, nor anything cuter than a mother loon carrying her chicks on her back.

We cleared the land and had a hole dug for the foundation. My father bought some lumber from an old barn that my uncle's brother had. This wood was very old, because it was one inch thick and anywhere from eight to twenty inches wide. The beams were four by eight inches, all solid and very hard to drive in a nail.

My father and uncle were both machinist, so when something was done, it was down to the smallest fraction of an inch. One of the things that they measured was the foundation. I do not remember the exact dimensions, but when they laid the cement blocks, measured them, and were done, the foundation was off by a sixteenth of an inch. This was tragic, but they left it. This was not the real tragedy though, which was when I went back to this camp forty years later and saw how the frost heaves and snow had destroyed their exact work. The people who had bought the camp had to jack the whole camp up and mount it on lally columns, so the original foundation was almost gone.

While we were building, a couple of things happened. One late fall day the temperature was about forty degrees in the morning. When we hear splashing, my uncle asks, "Who would be swimming on a morning like this?" We look out and see a huge old moose swimming across the lake.

Another morning I am up with my uncle and he says, "Let's go into Laconia for breakfast." Just as we get to the diner, a group of bikers roll in. One of them was a huge woman about six feet three inches, tall weighing at least 300 pounds. On the back of her black leather jacket is her name, Bertha. My uncle and I always had a good laugh when we talked about Big Bertha and her biker entourage.

My parents drove me to a party not too far from our camp. I was not enjoying the party, so I decided to walk home, seeing there were no phones up there.

Today I look back on this night as one of the strangest evenings I have ever had. It was a new moon, so because of this, it was pitch black. Close your eyes—that black. As I walk along the road, I stayed on the edge so I could feel the gravel by my left foot and pavement with my right. I was slowly walking back to camp, when I hear this strange sound. It was a rubbing, swishing sound. Then I hear two heavy thumps, followed by a groan and a pleading cry, "Help me, please help me!"

Now I don't know what to do. So I call back and the person again pleads for help. I come to the conclusion that I am OK and that the person calling for help really does need help.

What had happened was that the person I was hearing had been to a different party, where he was the entertainment, but had gotten drunk. The people at the party figured if they threw him into a cold lake, it would sober him up. When he climbed out of the lake, he gathered his guitar and amplifier and tried to head home. What I heard next was his wet corduroy pants rubbing together. The two heavy thumps was him dropping the steel guitar and amplifier on the road.

It was dark and he was still drunk and not doing well, so I asked him where he lived and helped him home. His father thanked me and offered to drive me home, but I said no thanks, my parents would be coming along shortly. I started walking on the road again and my parents did come along shortly.

Another time I worked with people that had friends in the same development that our camp was in and I was invited over there. They had a strange story to tell of going home one night on Route 111 through Exeter, New Hampshire, on the same night that there had been flying saucer sightings in that town.

They had a brand new Buick and as they were driving along, they encountered a bright light and remember nothing for the next twenty miles. The next morning when they went out to the car, they found that all the paint had cracked like an old car might do after forty or fifty years. They brought the car back to the dealer and he said that he had never seen anything like that before. Then they heard about all the UFO sightings in Exeter that night. They never saw anything but the bright light—but still, a strange coincidence.

While I am talking about UFO sightings, I told this story to my friend, Dick. I had traveled with him to Nova Scotia. He said he never believed in UFOs. However, when he got out of the service where he had been an MP, he received a job with Sikorsky Helicopter plant in Connecticut as a security officer. When he received a call of something strange going on by their power plant and was asked to go check it out, he went up the hill. When he came around the corner, here was this craft hovering over the generators. He said it was emitting a very bright light and as he watched, it just vanished before his eyes. He had never told anyone this story for fear they would think he was crazy!!! He only told me this story because I believed my friends from New Hampshire.

Another story in this same vein happened on my birthday, November 9, 1965. I am at work and the lights go out. My boss stations me at the door to turn people away, because we had lost power. I went online to refresh my memory as to what time it had happened, because I knew it had been my birthday. I quickly found the time had been 5:27 pm. The blackout covered the northeast and part of Canada. It had lasted thirteen hours and covered 80,000 square miles, affecting more than thirty million people. The reason given was that a 230 kilovolt transmission near Ontario caused the heavily loaded system to fail.

Here are some of the reports that were covered:

5 p.m., Newton, Massachusetts: Reported a bright fireball traveling east to west.

5 p.m., Jersey City, New Jersey: A bright object was seen moving north to south over Manhattan, New York. Then that object shot straight up at an extreme velocity.

5 p.m., A person on a flight between Syracuse and Rochester observed a bright light descend toward central New York.

5 p.m., Cornelius, New York: A housewife reported a huge dome-shaped object near a local substation five minutes before the blackout.

5 p.m., Cicero, New York:
A local pilot in a small plane reported seeing a huge bright light near high tension wires crossing the Mohawk River.

5 p.m., Personnel from the Sir Adam Beck Hydro Electric Power Plant, Ontario, Canada, reported four strange lights over the power plant.

5 p.m., Residents near Niagara Falls Power station reported seeing a huge glowing object hovering over the power station.

These were pillars of many communities, not a report from a drunk with an extra beer under his belt. These were posted by a columnist from *Syracuse New Times*.

All these reports were at 5 p.m. just before the great blackout!!! They all sounded exactly like my friends had described their encounters. There was a great deal written about this blackout and as I was refreshing my memory online. I found there have been incidents like this all over the world.

In later recollections of my road trip, I will talk about my visit to Roswell, New Mexico, and Area 51. Also, I will discuss my thoughts on how the ancients had the ability to move huge rocks and monoliths.

CHAPTER 8

Milkman

After leaving Demoulas and being home one day, our milkman asked if I needed a job. It seemed the dairy that delivered our milk needed a driver. So I went over and talked to the owner and got the job. When I started, I had a hard time not talking to everyone along the route. (Yes, I have always been full of hot air.) Some days I would leave home in the dark at sparrow fart, aka "O dark thirty," and come home in the dark. There was quite a long time, especially in the winter when it stayed dark so late in the morning and got dark so early in the evening, that I never saw my house in the daylight. I was working about one hundred hours a week and at one point, I got sick and being exhausted, I slept for almost forty-eight hours straight. I then realized I could not talk to everybody on my route as much as I did, although I still made friends with people and dogs.

I got to know one of my customer's kids very well. Years later, he still came to visit me at Sears, which was my next job.

I haven't changed the names of anybody I know that has died or I just do not use their names or I have gotten their permission to use them. But as I tell this story, you will see why I have changed *his* name. I will call him Tommy.

Tommy was a kid of about fifteen or sixteen years old—I delivered milk to his mother. He had many siblings and me being an only child, five or six kids seemed like a lot to me. He never talked about a father and I kind of got the feeling I was filling this void. He asked if he could come along and help me. Yes, this was probably illegal, but I felt sorry for him and let him come with me while I delivered to customers in his area. He would bring the milk to the icebox and I would give him a bottle of chocolate milk for his help. After I left the dairy a couple of years later, he comes into Sears and tells me his mother had moved around the corner, so he would come in to say hi every once in a while. One day he comes in and tells me he got a job driving customers for a local car dealer, making very good money.

A factory investigator comes in to check on a scam of the dealership filing false claims on warranties. The service manager at the dealership had just beaten a murder rap for killing his wife, so the owner hired him to whack the investigator by taking him for a ride. When the service manager comes back, the owner asks if the job is done and the service manager says yes. The owner then asked if there were any witnesses and the service manager says, only Tommy, the driver.

Thinking that Tommy was a little slow, the owner did not think this was a problem. However, just in case, the owner tells the service manager to whack Tommy, also. The service manager brings Tommy to a shed in Tyngsboro, Massachusetts, knocks him out, and sets the shed on fire—then leaves. Tommy comes to and immediately goes to the Tyngsboro police to tell them what happened.

Well, Tommy comes into the store while a government goon is standing there watching me and protecting him. I find this all extremely incredible and follow the story on the news.

Yes, the service manager and the owner of the dealership were found guilty and, strangely, I have never seen Tommy again. He is the only person I have ever known who has been put into the Witness Protection Program. I often wonder where Tommy is and what type of life he is living now.

One morning about 5 o'clock, I am out in the dairy loading my truck and a man running for congress is there greeting the employees. He is Brad Morse and the only politician I ever met that I really liked. I actually ended up working for him and helping on his campaign. However, even a good guy like him had some sneaky things going on. There was this one guy up from Washington who apparently was not supposed to be involved in the campaign, so I being a nobody and totally off the radar was given the job of driving him around.

While I am on the subject, I want to tell you my definition of a politician—a person who answers a question with an answer totally irrelative of the question. Brad Morse did not do that though. He did have one quality or trait that a politician has to have. That is remembering the name of everyone that they have ever met. As Brad walked through the dairy, he spotted and called by name a fellow that he had been stationed with in World War II twenty years before. This amazed the guy that I worked with.

I worked with another old timer who had fought in World War I in the cavalry. When he went over to Europe, he brought his own horse. When that horse was shot out from under him, he had to become a foot soldier.

One of the owners of the dairy was Earl Musgrave, but everybody called him Spook—even to his face. I asked why he was called Spook and he told me it was because he said so little and he could come up behind you without you knowing he was there.

It was at this time, I started going to a barber around the corner from my house. Forty-eight years and three locations later, he was the only person that ever cut my hair. He finally gave up on asking me how I wanted it. Now that I have moved to Florida, my wife is my barber and does a fantastic job. I should have done this years ago. Sorry, Fred. One day I asked him how old he was. He was the same age I am, but he said he was not going to retire. But the last time I was back visiting, the shop was closed. I guess my not going there put him out of business.

As the years went by, I learned we knew the same people—some famous, some infamous. Like all barbers, there was always something to talk about. The neat thing was, we had some great conversations about all the buffoonery going on politically. Our views on life were basically the same. I guess that is why you can go to the same barber for forty-eight years.

One of the guys I worked with had parents who owned a camp in Raymond, Maine. We went up there one week and he told me the tallest structure in the world was right there in Raymond. It was a TV tower built to send signals over the White Mountains at 1619 feet tall—the Empire State Building used to be the tallest at 1454 feet. This was true in 1963, but not any longer. The tallest structure is now Burj Khalifa in Dubai with 160 stories at 2722 feet tall.

As I was getting ready to leave, I found I had locked my keys in the car—something you can longer do. Dave's sister was there and she said, "I have a General Motors car, also. Let's see if my key will work." It did, but this I found strange.

While working at the dairy, what little time I had after work, I started playing pool at a local bowling alley in Reading, Massachusetts, which had pool tables. I found myself spending a lot of time and money there and decided I wanted to buy a pool table for my parents' basement. I mentioned this to the milk solicitor, who occasionally rode around the route with me to drum up new customers. He said he had a brother-in-law who had to sell an old 5 x 9 slate table. He had been running an after-hours pool room in his basement. When the guy did not come home, his wife would call this fellow's house looking for her husband. Sometimes he was there, but sometimes he was not. The wife finally said, "It's the pool table or me." He choose her and to show his good faith he had to disassemble the pool table. The solicitor set up a meeting with his brother-in-law and me.

He told me this table meant the world to his brother-in-law, but selling and getting a good home for his baby was more important than getting a high price. So what I should do when I got there was find out where it was disassembled and ask to see the cloth. Then I should compliment him on it not having any wear marks on the seams where the three pieces of slate meet. When his brother-in-law heard this question, he would know his baby would have a good home. I followed his advice, so he sold the table to me for one hundred fifty dollars.

Today I am told by those in the know that the table is worth several thousand dollars and I have probably spent at least that moving it and having it reassembled and leveled three times. It is the centerpiece of my bar. When I put it back together the last time, I weighed it. The total weight came to 1,000 pounds. I guess you can say I paid 15 cents a pound for it—one of the better deals in my lifetime. Not to mention that it came with twelve pool cues, a rack, and two sets of ivory balls. This I am told could be worth more than the table, along with a box of clamps to glue on the cue tips, a set of pills, and the straight pool beads.

The people I worked at the dairy with were great, but the dogs along the route were also memorable. One of my customers had this cute puppy. I was going to say cute little puppy, but every one that knows dogs that have big paws knows that means it's going to be a big dog. This dog's paws were huge. When I delivered milk, he would come running down their walk and jump up on me. I would set down my milk carrier and roll around on the ground with him for a minute or two. As time passed, I thought about how big he was getting—you see he was half great Dane and half St. Bernard. One day when he was basically full grown, but still a puppy at heart, and I guess you could say the same for me an adult, but a kid at heart, we ended up rolling around on the front lawn. A guy driving by sees this beast attacking a milkman, so he stops to help. I said it's OK—we're just playing. He looks at me like I was crazy, gets in his car, and drives off. Maybe he was right.

There was the good and the bad of not having any leash laws back then. I will tell the good, then the bad. One of the good was there was this poor dog that was left to roam all day long by himself. One day he hops up in my milk truck. With the doors open, there were no seats on either side—I drove standing up. The clutch was halfway down, the other half was the brake. I balanced my right foot on my heel, pressing down on my toes teetering back the gas. The truck would slow down and I kind of balanced myself, holding on to the gear shift and obviously the steering wheel. This I know sounds tricky but it took me no time at all to get used to. The dog could come and go as he wanted and I let him ride around in the neighborhood with me. At the end of the day, I would let him off where I met him, because he seemed to be well fed— just left to roam during the day. As time went by, I let him ride a little further. Finally, after two or three months, he was riding the entire route with me on the days I went to his area.

One day a cop stops and asks, "Is that your dog?" I say, "No, he's with me just for the ride."

Again, I get the crazy look and he says, "Well, you do not have any control over him."

I said, "Sure I do. As soon as I start the truck, he will be back on it." I start the truck, the dog hops on, and I drive off. The cop just stands there shaking his head.

Another dog that drove a small part of the route was a basset hound. He also loved to ride along with me, with his floppy ears blowing in the wind. One of my deliveries was up a dirt road— at least, when it was not raining. One day it was raining and the road was full of mud puddles. When I get to the bottom and look over, to my horror, the basset is not there. I stop and look back up the hill. Here is this little guy covered in mud, with his little legs carrying him as fast as they could, trying to catch up with me. After I realized he was all right, I thought what I had just witnessed was very comical, but I never let him ride with me again. I did not want to be responsible for the demise of a pure-bred basset. I liked the little guy too much.

My last good story—and it will not sound good initially—is at another one of my stops. It had a nasty German Shepherd and I always worried if he was out. If he was in, I could deliver the milk in a minute, but if he was out, I would slink up the walk holding the milk in one hand and fending off the dog who was growling at my milk carrier with barred teeth with the other. This is one of the few dogs I have ever been afraid of.

His owner happened to see my plight, while I was trying to deliver her milk. She came to the door with some cookies and said, "Just give him a couple of cookies and you will be his friend for life." Sure enough, from then on, I always brought some cookies with me just for this stop—he was my friend as long as I delivered there.

The bad story of not having a leash law was one of the worst days of my life. However, for my stories to be complete, I have to tell it, as much as I hate to. One day like all the others, I am delivering the milk and I come back to the truck, score my delivery, and start up the truck. When I start to drive away. the back right tire rolls over something. I stop and hear this wailing of a dog who crawls to the customer's back step and dies.

I was beside myself with apologies and grief. The customer calmly said, "Do not worry about it. He had it coming, because he always slept under a car's rear tire. I knew it was going to happen someday." However, this did not make me feel much better. I kind of wanted to ask the guy why he let him continue doing it, but I just left.

Not a half hour later, I am driving along and a dog runs out beside the right front tire and chases the truck. I was kind of used to this, because this dog had chased my truck many times before. I slow down till I got out of his area and he had tired of this game that he played with every car that had come down his street. This day he changed the game and with a spurt of energy he got in front of the tire and turned and faced it head on. At the angle of where I was, I did not see this game change and rode over him head to tail.

Watching this horror were the kids who owned the dog. The kids went screaming into the house and the dog went wailing into some bushes. It seems that their father was a policeman for the town, so he comes out with a police pistol. I did not know if he was going to shoot me or the dog. He walked into the bushes and put the dog out of his misery. Then, he proceeded to come over to me and apologize for having to see what he had just done, saying he knew it was going to come to that.

I did not understand how people could think this way. Now I just want this day to end, but it is not over yet. I am almost home, when from behind a hedge, a dog runs out in front of my car and before I could stop, it was over—the worst day of my life.

Another story of death in the pet world is my great-aunt Ruth, who had two parakeets, Petey and Tweety. One was yellow and one was blue—together they would make quite a racket.

Finally, my great-aunt decided that she should have only one. So she gives my father Petey and we bring him home. In the process of catching Petey, my father pulls out his tail feathers, so Petey comes to our house tailless. At this time, we had a cat named Friskey, who spent the better part of his day eyeing Petey. Whenever we left the house, we had to put the cat out.

I came home from work one day and changed my clothes to go out to meet some friends. However, I forget to put Friskey out again. Poor Petey did not have a chance. The cat had leaped from the top of the TV to the bird cage and got the water holder out of the cage. The bird had somehow escaped through this water hole, but the poor bird did not have a chance without tail feathers. There were feathers in every room of the house. I never knew that a little bird could have so many feathers. It took a couple of days to find a small trace of the body.

About a week later, my great-aunt decided that Tweety was missing Petey and wanted him back. My father, knowing that my great-aunt could not handle the news of Petey's demise, goes out and buys another Petey. When we bring Petey number two over to her, she was amazed at how fast the tail feathers grew back—Tweety was thrilled for Petey's return.

Another strange story concerns the milk solicitor when he had a new customer for me in Woburn, Massachusetts on Montvale Street. My instructions were to just go to the back porch and put the milk in the refrigerator. However, there was no refrigerator on the back porch. The problem with this delivery was for some reason like a lot of towns in New England that use the same name for different streets. Woburn had several Montvales—Street, Avenue, Road, Lane, and Court. My Montvale instructions had the wrong Montvale label. I ended up going into the kitchen, where I saw the refrigerator, but not the girl standing there in her underwear ironing a dress. I apologized and quickly left. On my return to the dairy, I learned the correct house address, so I handed out some free milk and all was forgiven. I do not know if Woburn has renamed its streets for the safety of emergency vehicles. I do know several other towns have changed their names for this same reason.

During this time I was dating a girl from Winchester, Massachusetts. Coming home I went through an intersection that I heard about on the news the next morning. The police had found a nude body that had been dropped within fifteen minutes of when I had driven through this intersection. This was during the time of the

Boston gang wars, so I often wondered what would have happened if I had witnessed this drop.

It was at this time I get a call from Uncle Sam and I go into South Boston terminal for my physical. While going through this process, one of the guys in front of me is acting like he is deaf. The doctor sends him into a small hearing test room with a glass window. He is supposed to respond with a hand signal when he can hear the test frequency and not respond when there is no sound. He does not respond at the right times, so he figured he had outsmarted the doctor giving the test. When the doctor is done, he turns away from the guy and says, "OK, you can go now." The guy was out of the room in a flash, but the doctor turned around and simply says, "Get back in there and take it again."

After taking my physical and passing, I am told that I can enlist in any branch of the service I wanted, instead of getting drafted into the army. I opt to join the coast guard and have to go for another physical. Going through that physical, the coast guard doctor finds that I have a heart murmur, which should have been caught by the army doctor. The coast guard doctor overruled my army classification of lA and I was told that I could not serve in any branch of the service.

CHAPTER 9

Britannica

Finding that I should not be doing heavy physical work, I leave the milk route, which was very physical, and get a job selling encyclopedias. This was the strangest company for which I have ever worked, but the education I received in selling was very good. However, the education I got in life was peculiar, to say the least.

I have to omit some of the stuff I saw happening. Although, I will say it was where I learned what the word perverted meant, because one salesmen was saying that one of the guys who was not there anymore was perverted. I went home and looked up the word in the dictionary. The best definition was, "One who has deviated from the normal." If it had been a dictionary with pictures of the person like this, it would have been his picture. The fellow they called perverted would brag about his escapades with a nun in Portland, Maine. I

did not know if his stories were true or if they were just part of his perverted personification.

While he was in Portland, my boss would call his wife and have phone sex with her on the speakerphone with everybody listening. Looking back on this, I do not know if it was for real or if they were just trying to shock the new kid in the office. I do know it was the first time I had ever seen or heard a speakerphone.

One day my boss' Cadillac is in the garage for a tune-up and he asks if he could borrow my car to take his secretary out to lunch. I use the word "lunch" loosely, because when I get my car back, my black interior was full of white shoe polish scuffs from the secretary's white shoes. Even the headliner had scuffs.

Another fellow who worked there never came into the office before calling ahead to see if any bill collectors or police were there looking for him. He was paying—or not paying—support for three wives. I did not know the count on how many kids.

He claimed to have been Esther Williams sales manager for her swimsuit business. He also claimed to have coined the phrase, "Everybody out of the pool." I cannot remember which famous actor it was, but I do remember he was on Johnny Carson's show when they were joking about how this phrase came about. It seems that they used to have pool parties and Esther's bathing suits were not being used. Of course, it seems *nobody's* suits where being used. It was this fellow who stood watch when Esther's neighbors called the police to complain. Then he would call out, "Everybody out of the pool!" This is one of those stories I said I could not verify, but seeing the *Carson Show* and knowing this guy, it all really did fit.

This fellow had lost his pilot's license for buzzing the Hyannis

Airport when there was a no-fly zone, because President Kennedy's plane was coming into the Hyannis Airport. He also did not have a license, so they would send him out to train the new sales people as they were hired.

I was told to take him with me to Newburyport, Massachusetts, so I could learn how to sell encyclopedias. After three hours, this one customer told him to get out of his house, but the guy said he was not leaving. I thought they were going to come to blows, but the customer finally bought the encyclopedias, just to get rid of him. However, he canceled the order the very next morning.

Another time, we drove to Boston for a sales meeting. When we went into a coffee shop and waited in line, one of the fellows proceeded to show us how to have sex with an obese woman. This was a very embarrassing moment.

At another meeting, we are driving down Route 128, following the boss in his Cadillac. Another one of the guys was on his bumper in his VW, honking his horn like the Caddy was in his way.

The fellow that I was driving around and supposed to be learning from said he would buy me lunch to show his appreciation for me driving. After we left, he told me not to go back there again. When I asked why, he said he very rarely ever paid for a meal there.

I was still trying to see some way of working with all these scum bags, when I had three calls that just made me throw in the towel and quit.

The first call was to a third floor walkup in the poorest part of Lynn, Massachusetts. You have probably not heard the saying that most people who live north of Boston have heard:

Lynn, Lynn, the city of sin
You never come out the way you came in

You ask for water, they give you gin
The girls say no, but they always give in

If you're not bad, they won't let you in
It's the damnedest city I've ever been in

Lynn, Lynn, the city of sin
You never come out the way you came

This mother had hardly anything, but she did not want her children to be tied to this heritage. She wanted her daughter to have a chance at being educated and living in a nicer city and not tied to this ditty, as she had been all her life. I was trained to tell her that a personal library could take care everything that the daughter needed and more. She actually pleaded and cried to buy the set. I have never felt more guilty over a sale in my life. You just cannot tell somebody that they cannot afford what you are selling.

The next two calls were in northern Maine. I was not making a lot of money in this profession, because you had to buy all your leads. Yes, you could sit at a phone and cold call hundreds of people a day with a scripted sales pitch or you could spend three dollars and buy a lead from the Sunday comic pages. If you paid five dollars, the lead came from a magazine and for ten dollars, it came from a professional magazine sent out to doctors and lawyers. Very rarely would I buy a five or a ten-dollar lead.

A three-dollar lead sent me to Maine. When I got there, I could not afford a room, so I went to the local police station and asked where I could sleep in my car without bothering anybody. The cop at the desk said I could stay in one of the cells or go down to the park and sleep in its parking lot and he would let the guys know I was there. I chose the park. I woke up the next morning with the sun rising and a nice cool breeze. I was well-rested and wondered what I was going to do till the town woke up. Then I noticed a huge swing set and went over and sat down. Soon I was swinging back and forth. I start going higher and higher and as I am almost ready to launch myself into the next universe, that's when the cruiser shows up to check on me. Yes, another embarrassing incident, but this time, a funny moment.

My call in northern Maine was with a potato farmer who did not have a library nearby, so he wanted something better than farming for his kids. This made more sense to me than the lady in Lynn.

He bought the encyclopedia set from me with a postdated check and instructions to call before cashing it. He wanted to wait until the potato crop had been harvested and he knew he had the money to cover the check.

My next call heading south was with a Great Northern lumberjack. I went to the gate and asked how I could find Pierre. They said he was working up the road about thirty-five to forty miles away. Now I had already driven about fifty miles to get this far, so I asked how I would find him there. They described his truck. About forty miles down this dirt lumber road, I come to his truck.

I got out and hear a chainsaw in the woods, so I take my briefcase and off I trudge. Coming across two guys, I ask which one is Pierre.

One guy says, "I am." I introduce myself and say that I am from Encyclopedia Britannica and that he had sent in a request to receive information on buying a set.

Well, it seems that the other fellow thought I had just told the funniest joke of his life and could not stop laughing. Finally, he gained some composure and admitted he had sent in the lead as a funny joke. Pierre could not read or write and could barely speak English. After entertaining Pierre's partner and driving 180 miles with nothing but a post-dated check to show for my three-day trip to Maine, I head for home with my tail between my legs, totally downhearted.

CHAPTER 10

Sears

The next morning after I get home, my mother in her ultimate wisdom says she saw that Sears was looking for sales people for their new store in Lowell, Massachusetts.

The rest is history and I spent thirty-four years with a great company—at least in the beginning. Toward the end, it started to slide, but then all good things must come to an end.

Training back then was different than today—when opening a new store, they sent in a team of people to train us. Training was done in an old warehouse behind the site of the new store and the VFW hall across the street. Out of a month of training, the one thing that was drilled into us was that if a customer wanted to return something, you took it back, because the sign over the door said, "Satisfaction guaranteed or your money back." An example of this philosophy was a friend of a corporate executive of Sears, who asked him why Sears did not sue *Readers Digest* for their article on how to return things at Sears. The executive said to his friend, "Why sue them when we wrote the article?"

My technical training was more intense. I had the background, because as strange as the encyclopedia people were, they did know how to train people in the art of selling. Without giving too much detail on selling and to my knowledge, it was not covered in any college course—at least back then it wasn't. One part of encyclopedia training was—and it was on a training record—you do several things. The first and most important thing you do after giving your pitch is you shut your F—king mouth. This must be encyclopedia language that the salesmen understand.

The second thing you do is put the contract in front of the customer and accidentally drop your pen on the floor in front of the person. If they pick it up, they will generally hold the pen for a few minutes and inadvertently sign the contract.

Another ploy is to keep asking questions to which the customer must say yes. While going down the Yes road, you throw in, "Would you like to own this set?" They are so used to saying, "Yes," you end up selling whatever you had been pitching. After rereading my closing format, I never really thought that there was enough material to make this a college course. It is this simple though.

My training was not so much how to sell, because they hired me for that "so-called" experience. My training of the month was how to design kitchens and explain the quality of the product. I felt much better selling kitchens than encyclopedias.

The fellow that was hired with me was a carpenter who had built and installed kitchens all his life. We made a great team. I had the selling experience with no installation and he had the installation experience with no selling. We got along well and helped each other.

One thing I will always remember about Ed was that when someone asked about our best cabinets and how much they cost, he would always start off talking the same way saying, "Speaking of our cost …

Then, Ed would simply ask, "Well, Little Lady, have you got your feet firmly planted on the floor?" Then, he would bowl 'em over with the price. Ed could not understand why they would walk away. My boss and I finally got him to be a little softer on his approach.

Our boss, Warren, was bigger than life in more ways than one. He was about six foot five inches tall and weighed about three hundred pounds. He could give the best impression of Jackie Gleason's "… and away we go" or "One of these days to the moon, Alice." Warren took everything in stride, including his giving up on trying to have a son after five girls.

He had a great sense of humor until one day he got stuck in the store freight elevator, which had a double set of doors. The inner door was a steel cage and once that closed, the outer solid door would also close. Only when the both doors were closed would the elevator work.

Warren got on the elevator with some kitchen supplies and the inner cage door closed, but the solid outer door jammed open. The elevator doors would not open or close. There Warren was, like a caged animal—no, he was a caged animal. He roared and paced back and forth for four hours until the repair man showed up. Warren did not find this waiting at all funny, especially after somebody put up a sign that said, "Please do not feed the animal." From his view, he could not see the sign, so it made him even madder, as everybody came by to see him and his sign.

I had a customer come in to confront my boss and me. He wanted an electric cooktop and I designed it into the kitchen, but failed to ask him if he had a 220-volt service, which it needed or it was going to cost another six hundred dollars to run the line. Today it would be a *lot* more. The customer was a nice little old man about four feet eight inches tall and weighing maybe one hundred ten pounds. It was amazing to see this man confronting my boss—remember his six foot five inch frame and his three hundred thirty pounds weight. It was not funny then, but to look back on it with the little guy flailing his two canes in the air, it was a memorable sight. Warren was a diplomat and negotiated a fifty/fifty settlement, telling the customer that it would have cost him six hundred dollars to do this and he was getting it for three hundred dollars. Warren was very good at making the customer feel that he won. This to me is what a good boss should do, but for myself, he just shrugged his shoulder and called it an honest mistake. Some men would have ranted for weeks. I liked Warren.

The most laid-back guy I have ever known ran the next department. On a hot summer day when there were no customers, he would put up a sign by the phone saying to call this number if you need help. It was for the bar at the VFW across the street. Yes, things were different back then.

In this vein, I do not like to talk about it, but like my story about the dogs, another bad day comes to pass—or should I say another bad night. If I am going to give you my life's journey, I have to tell all of the stories, good *and* bad.

I had been having some very good sales and winning several store sales contests, so I decided to go out with a couple of my friends and celebrate. At the end of the evening of celebrating, it seems the local police noticed that I was not driving too well. The rest is history. The next morning, the desk officer comes to my cell and tells me I have visitors. I am brought out to find to my dismay that my parents are there, because they had heard about my adventure on the local radio station.

My father tells me I have to be in court at 10:00 o'clock and he will see me there. At 10:00 the judge asks if I have a lawyer. I look at my father and he gives me a look that says you made your bed, now sleep in it. My father was used to doing this, having been in the navy with many men under his command, so he was kind of understanding. After paying my fine and walking back to the car where my mother is waiting in complete disgust, he simply says, "When you get in the car, roll down the window and do not breathe on your mother."

The next year was hard, because I could no longer be on the road selling, having just lost my license. I talked my way into selling clothes and getting an apartment within walking distance of the store.

My circle of friends changed a little and the next year was basically going where everybody else wanted to go. One night I was up to my old tricks, where I was not driving, but I had a few drinks. One of our old haunts was a Chinese restaurant. It seems that the entertainment for the waiters was to give the drunken customers a dose of breathtaking hot sauce. I put the hot sauce on my food and it took my breath away so badly that I felt like I was dying. This was their form of entertainment. The China man just stood there and laughed, as I am trying to draw what I felt was my last breath. My friends get me out of there and as they are driving me home to my apartment, I decided to get out of the car at the stoplight in front of the police station. I go in to file a complaint against the China man who tried to kill me. The first thing the desk sergeant asks is, "Are you driving?"

I said, "No, why?" Well the desk sergeant calls the officer in charge and he comes to the desk and asks what seems to be the problem. I proceed to tell him about my near-death experience with the sadistic China man. He humors me and takes all the information and then asks me again if I was driving. I said no and he says all right, you can go.

I have stated earlier there are times when I am not the brightest bulb in the room. I ended up at the same Chinese restaurant the next night like nothing had happened the previous night, because I rarely hold a grudge. I walk into the Chinese restaurant and my hot sauce friend is standing there. He comes up to me and asks very apologetically how Paul is tonight. It seems the Lowell police had actually followed up on my complaint, so we all had a good laugh.

During this time of selling clothing, I would occasionally go out for lunch and have a couple of beers. While I was there, everybody kept on saying, "Oh, let's have one more." At the time, it seemed like a great idea. When I got back, my boss is standing there with a glum look on his face as he says, "They want to see you up in the store manager's office." As I start to leave, he says, "Oh by the way, I think you should chew on a couple of these." He hands me two breath mints. I walk into the store manager's office thinking, *I have used up all my nine lives like my pet cat, Friskey.* The manager says, "It's OK, Paul, you can go. We have resolved the problem." It seems that the trainee from Chicago would sell a sweater and take the money, then put it into his pocket and give the customer a no sales ring slip.

Well, security was watching him and when confronted, he said he was just holding the money for me, so I could ring up the sale when I got back and get the commission. When I was gone so long they just continued to grill him, till he finally admitted that he was pocketing the money and I had nothing to do with this scam.

The security guy was super smooth and he seemed to be flirting and putting the moves on a cute girl. He was with her a couple hours a day in the coffee shop or in her section where she worked. One day he was just walking her out to her car, but when they got to the car, he asked to see the sales slips of the packages she was carrying. She had bogus slips that did not cover what she was carrying out. The rumors of the love affair were over.

I do not know if it was the area the store was in or just that I worked there and heard all the crime stories first-hand. On almost every holiday when the store was closed, someone would come down and throw a rock through the glass door closest the TV department and carry out a couple of the best sets. It took five to ten minutes for the police to get there, but by that time, the thief was gone. Finally, they just blocked up the door by the TV department.

There was an opening from the upstairs warehouse into the dumpster that was locked every night, but they never checked to see what was in the dumpster. The stock men would throw whatever they wanted into it and come back at night to dig it out. TVs were the merchandise of choice, but they finally caught these guys.

However, there was one thief I do not think they ever caught. Every night the girl at the jewelry counter would put all the diamonds into a tool box and bring them over to the store safe. One night, she had put all the diamonds into the tool box, when a fellow comes along and asks to see a particular watch. Then he decides against it and leaves. She turns around to get the tool box and it was gone—all 10,000 dollars of it.

They grilled the poor girl eight hours the next day. It was really their fault for not having somebody with her each night, which they did every night after that.

While I was just standing there, I see the security guy chasing a guy out the front door, so I walk over to the side door to watch the chase. The thief comes around the corner and is heading toward me. The security guy yells, "Stop him!"

I simply raised my hand and yelled, "Stop!" Strangely he did, so we recovered the camera he had stolen. I look back at this and think, he could have shot or stabbed me or simply just kept running. I do not know why he stopped.

One evening the security guy comes and asks if I will walk over to the bank with him, to deposit the days take. Since the bank is right next door, I did not think anything of this, so I said, "Sure." When we get to the bank, I see the slip for how much was being deposited. The crooks of that day did not know that the deposit was for 60,000 dollars. That was a lot of money back then, to say nothing about today.

It was deposited by two unarmed guys—though the security guy might have been packing. He did tell me that when he went to meetings, they would make all the security people check their weapons before they went into the room.

There always seemed to be something strange going on in the store. One day I went into the men's room to see a kid standing there soaking toilet paper and throwing it against the wall and onto the ceiling. I told him to stop and he just kept on doing it. Then he said, "You cannot touch me, because you work here."

Just then I hear a toilet flush and a guy walks out of a stall. He gives the kid a hard back hand that sets him up against the wall. The guy simply said to the kid, "I don't work here," and walks out. The kid was not that clever, because he could have still blamed me and I could not have proved otherwise.

Another time a woman comes running out of the lady's room saying that there was a man in one of the stalls. The security guy asks, "How do you know?" She said, "I have been married for forty-five years, so I know what a man sounds like." When he goes in, he finds that it was simply an old guy who went into the wrong restroom.

We were a retail store so I should relate some sales stories.

You never knew what the store manager was going to come up with next for a sales promotion. This was one of his craziest. He did not go through corporate for this one. He had ordered 10,000 shirts to sell at two dollars apiece. He said we had one week to sell them at two dollars a shirt. That came out to 2,000 boxes of shirts, stacked four high and two deep in every aisle in the store—anybody could sell them.

Toward the middle of the week, when the sale was supposed to be over, corporate got wind of it and sent somebody out to check on our progress. The trailer that the shirts had come in was gone, so with little advanced notice the remaining shirts were put on the freight elevator. When the visitors were upstairs, they sent the shirts downstairs and when they went downstairs we sent the shirts upstairs. After the visit, when all the shirts had been sold, Lowell had sold more shirts than any other store in the country, with corporate still scratching their heads on how.

As you can tell, our store manager was always thinking of a way to have a different sales promotion. Here's a couple that went awry.

There was the time that he decided to have Xmas in July. All the kids started to cry to their mothers that they wanted Xmas presents and where was Santa. But worst was the winter carnival. He talked a carnival company into coming to set up in the parking lot without checking on the extended weather report—not that they were that accurate back then. As soon as the carnival was set up, we got hit with an eighteen-inch snowstorm, followed by several more storms. He didn't do that again.

Probably the strangest sale was when a fellow comes in Xmas Eve to buy a sewing machine for his wife. He walks in the back door about 4:45—we were closing at 5:00 o'clock. He picks out his sewing machine, but back then all approvals had to be called in and the lines were tied up. The man starts acting very nervous. Security is called and the man is assured we will not lock up till we get the approval. The man said, "That's not the problem," watching his watch nervously. His concern was that he had stopped his train on a main trunk line from Portland, Maine, to Providence, Rhode Island, in back of the store, because by the time he got back to Providence, all the stores would be closed. And the next scheduled train was at 5:30!! The salesman gets the approval at 5:20 and the man is back on his train at 5:25 and rolling at 5:28. All of us are standing outside watching as that next freight train rolled threw at 5:32!!!

Right after Xmas. I am at a club on Nuttings Lake in Billerica, Massachusetts, to listen to a friend who was playing drums in a band. When I come out, the police are there. It seems that they had been chasing a car that had plowed into my car. They asked me to come to the station to fill out a report. When I got there, they put me in the same room as the guy who hit my car and left the two of us alone. When they come back about fifteen minutes later and looked at me, they asked, "Why didn't you beat the shit out of the asshole?" This I thought was strange. For some reason, I thought they wanted me to do what they could not do to him.

Everybody at Sears golfed, so sociably I went along with them. I really never quite understood the concept of grown men walking around chasing a little white ball. I guess it goes back to the saying, "The only difference between men and boys is the price of their toys." Or possibly they just needed an excuse to get to the nineteenth hole. I guess this was the reason for the four hours of abuse.

I even took up lessons. This was a financial waste of money that I will never see again. After every time I went out, I would end up with a bad headache. Headaches were something I rarely ever had then or now, so I figured there had to be a cause. Whether it was the pain of playing the game or being out in the sun, I never thought the problem could be what I was eating.

As time went on, I figured it out, because I would get headaches after meals and no golf. The common ingredient was Bermuda red onions. After a round of golf, I would have a hamburger with a slice of onion. I also would have a salad with Bermuda red onions at a friend's camp in New Hampshire. We would have shish kabobs with the Bermuda reds. I had eaten and loved Bermuda red onions all my life, but apparently you can develop an allergy to them as you age. The question is how to prove this? Abstention is the answer.

I went three months without any Bermuda reds, then ate a hamburger with a slice on top. That was it. I now knew I had an allergy. A strange side note to this story concerns a cousin who starts having these headaches and she remembered my experience. She decides to eliminate the raw red onions and her headaches disappeared. Must run in the family!

I will not talk much about golfing because you could probably tell I am not a golfer, aka wacker-baller! I am amazed at what people pay for a round of golf now—yes, I am dating myself—it was three to five dollars a round when I gave it up. It is not my idea of fun walking around in the rough whatever its depth looking for a little white ball and trying not to disturb the rattlesnakes and copperheads. Yes, it is strange, because in my retirement I am living in a golfing community only because I liked the house. I mention this since the clubhouse has a six-foot rattlesnake mounted directly over the registration desk and several alligators have been pulled out of the water hazards.

Another thing that amazes me is what people spend on cigarettes, which is another thing that used to make me sick. I gave them up when I went to visit a friend in the hospital with a hole in his throat from cancer. That fact and the price hike to thirty cents a pack made me give up that habit. I had many friends on my Catalina 30 sailboat and they would ask how I could afford such a boat as they were lighting up their cigarettes. I told them they could have the boat of their dreams if they stopped smoking, and they kept their boat under 30 feet. The big ones cost more than a pack of cigarettes a day. Maybe if you are a two pack a day person, you could get a bigger boat or pay the slip fees and fuel.

I tell them to do the math. Six dollars a pack for a year is $2190 times thirty years is $65,700. Now you are probably going to say there are other costs and you are right. Now I am going to tell you how a frugal Yankee who likes to sail covered the cost of his pleasure. Yes, I am thrifty and have brown-bagged my lunch all my life. That kind of lunch cost about $3 and it's pretty hard to spend less than $10 on a regular lunch today. The difference is $7 and on a five-day work week $35 and say you have a month off, you work 48 weeks, that is $1680, enough to cover insurance, slip, and gas fees. Now you have to keep out of the high rent marinas, but you should get the idea of where I am going with this. If boating is not your thing, a lot of other hobbies or cars work with this math of Yankee frugality.

I have to tell the story about having been in a partnership with a close friend with a boat that I will talk about later. When we sold that boat, I bought the Catalina on my own. He said he would like to charter and pay to take it out. So, I take my first year's expenses and divide it by the number of times I left the dock and it comes out to $300.00 a day. I couldn't charge him that much. It shows that if you are only an occasional boater, it's much cheaper to go with an organization like Freedom Boat. Later on, I read about another fellow with a Catalina 30 who made the same calculation of three hundred dollars a day. Sometimes it's cheaper to rent a boat or a car and get it out of your system, rather than being tied down to it for life by buying it.

One of the guys I worked with who left a significant impression on me was Gary. He was a character. He had a love of life and a huge, if strange, sense of humor. One day the store organized a fishing trip. It is not just the guys this time, since several of the women wanted to come along. The fishing charter was out of Rye, New Hampshire, and it was a pretty nasty day. It was overcast, cold, foggy, and the seas were fairly rough. Four of the women went into the main cabin to have lunch and, as they started eating their sandwiches, Gary walked up to them with a mouthful of Dinty Moore beef stew, and, making believe he was sick, "blows" lunch all over the table. This is bad enough, but he apologizes, and proceeds to scoop up the stew and shove it back into his mouth. Now the women have no desire to eat their sandwiches, so Gary asks if he can have them.

Gary was a big Dr. Hook fan, so one day when he asks me if I wanted to go to a Dr. Hook concert,. I said, "Sure!" We got there early and he tells the usher he is a relative of the warm-up band. That gets us a seat up front. When Dr. Hook comes onstage, we do not move and nobody notices, so we had front row seats. When we left, it is snowing pretty heavily. When we get to Gary's, he realizes he had somehow picked up a section of a neighbor's chain link fence. It had attached to the rear bumper of his car, so like a good neighbor, Gary returned the fence.

Gary's kids were allergic to most animals with fur, so he bought a $700 cockatoo. The bird rode on his shoulder while he was home. One day, not thinking, he went out to his van with that bird on his shoulder as usual. The bird must have figured that now was his time to head south like all birds, so suddenly there was $700 on the wing. His kids missed the bird, but Gary could not bring himself to buy another one.

Instead, he did a little research and found out that people with fur allergies can generally tolerate skunks. He bought one and took it home. That skunk was really like a pet dog. He'd had the scent gland removed, of course, but it still had a strange, musky smell that was tolerable. The thing that surprised me was how that skunk felt— solid muscle, like a rock. Now my wife was out of town, so I invited Gary to my house with the skunk. I took some pictures of it in the living room. When my wife came home, I showed her the pictures, but she knew that Gary had a skunk, so I didn't fool her.

The Sears crowd was always thinking of a new adventure and one of the guys came up with the idea of going on a whitewater raft trip up in Maine. We sign up ten people and off we go—Gary was one of the guys. I remember waking up in the middle of the night and seeing his van driving through the woods with his headlights bouncing in the trees. The next morning, I found out he had wanted to go to Canada, but if he had, he would have missed the raft trip.

That evening one of the bosses was sleeping in his car. The guys had opened his door and started poking him with a stick and yelling, "Bear, bear!" Poor guy almost had a heart attack! It took him a long time to see the humor in this.

This boss was a pretty good mark for a practical joke. Another time he was waiting on a customer when one of the guys sneaked up in back of him. Then—how can I say this nicely? He laid one of the worst smelling farts you can imagine. As he turned to walk his customer to the cash register, he hit a wall of pungency that is impossible to describe.

Periodically this boss would have a visit from OSHA, so he has to walk the floor with the agent. As he is standing there going over the checklist, I walk past the two of them and give a fake trip by kicking my right toe into my left heel. I almost fall on my face as I continue. Then I stop and look as the OSHA guy is trying to see what I tripped on.

Our last raft trip had gotten so much notoriety that we had fifty people who wanted to go on this one. We finally found a raft company that said they could handle us. However, we could not find a place to stay, so we went to the local police department. When we asked about camping, they gave us permission to camp on their fairgrounds.

The next morning, we got up to cook breakfast, but nobody could get a fire going, so somebody got the bright idea of going to the local diner. The operative word here is "local," which means the regular clientele was about ten people. When we walk in, the cook runs to the phone and calls a relative, telling him to bring eggs, bacon, bread, and help. They took care of all of us in about an hour.

This trip was quite a group of people coming from all up and down the East Coast, with some flying into the local airport. My wife's cousin from England said he wanted to experience some of the new world's wild adventures. We gave him that in spades with Gary being along. They came from all walks of life—I believe it was one of the most unusual trips that many of us had ever had. It was not only this trip that welded lasting friendships, but it certainly helped.

I mentioned my wife's cousin. Well, we met through Sears, but she did not work there. One of the women I worked with was sort of a party animal and I got invited to the party—or should I say zoo? While I was there, I met her roommate, aka "future wife." I cannot remember nor can she what I broke, but I broke something and as an apology, I told her I would take her out. She then went around and checked with one of the girls I had gone out with who dared her to go out with me. The rest is history.

Our first date was at Lenny's on the Turnpike on Route One in Danvers, Massachusetts. Lenny's was a dive, but a famous one. Some of the people we saw there were Dizzy Gillespie, Buddy Rich, and Skitch Henderson, to name a few. Skitch did not play there—he just popped in and looked around and said what a dive. That just added to the atmosphere. So our strange dating began. You are probably wondering why I said it was strange. It seems everywhere we went that first year later burned down—Lenny's, Blimstrom's, and even the 1800 club in east Boston. Then we took a ride on the cog railroad up Mount Washington. It never had an accident in over one hundred years, but it derailed a month after we rode on it. It was like I was Indiana Jones and everything was falling apart behind us.

However, good things were also happening. Neil Armstrong, Buzz Aldrin, and Mike Collins had just landed on the moon. When they returned, I heard there was going to be a ticker-tape parade in New York. This was like my cup of coffee in New York—it just seemed like something I had to be a part of, but it was more exciting than my coffee.

When I arrived, I somehow found a parking garage and followed the crowds to the parade route. As I was standing there, I started talking to a guy who said he was from Boston. After the astronauts had passed, he told me where to get a good picture from a bridge further down the parade route.

The crowds quickly separated us, but I followed his suggestion to go to the bridge they were to pass under and sure enough, I got some great photos. Later as I was trying to get back to my car, I bumped into this same guy and was able to thank him for his suggestion.

Afterwards, I heard that this ticker-tape parade was the last great parade of this kind, because ticker-tapes no longer were being used as much and a lot of the windows in the skyscrapers would no longer be able to be opened. I still look back at this day as one of the most exciting events in history that I was able to witness.

Later in life I met some people who were part of the space program. They were just everyday people doing a job, but to me they are really extraordinary people joined together to do extraordinary things.

This is what America is all about. Since then I have visited the Space Center in Huntsville, Alabama, and Cape Canaveral in Florida. It never stops amazing me that it all started on a sand dune in Kitty

Hawk, North Carolina, where I occasionally vacation.

As I start dating my future wife, I learn that her mother's side of the family is in England, while her father's side of the family lives in Marietta, Ohio. As time goes on, I decide that I should drive out to meet her parents and four siblings. Summer comes and she flies home to visit them, but I tell her I will drive out. After 750 miles and sixteen hours later, I arrive in Marietta, Ohio.

Even though I had lived along the whole East Coast, I had never felt serenity like this town had. It was the beginning of the Midwest and at one time had been an outpost to the westward push. Then and even now riverboats ply the Ohio River moving goods up and down the river.

Though as peaceful as it appears, these industries were and still are screwing their help. My future father-in-law was a vice president of one of these companies. When the owner's son graduated from college, they came to John, aka future father-in-law, and said that his position now required a college degree. Therefore, he would have to step down and be the plant manager. John could not swallow his pride, so he just quit. He found a job in the south shortly after this.

A side note to all of this is a couple of years later, he became terminally ill. I had to go and tell his new boss that he could no longer work for him. That man thought so much of him and told me that John had done so much for his company and its employees that he knew he would be back. He said, "I will pay him till he comes back." My mother-in-law got a regular check until he passed over a year later. The strange ending to all of this was the company that my father-in-law had done so much for the owner and its employees was a casket company!!!

I cannot remember actually asking John for his blessing, but I think it was kind of understood what was going on and a date was set for July 4, 1970. When else could an American flag get married? We really chose this date so everybody could come, because they all had the day off. In the future, we would always have a day off on our anniversary and it would be an easy day to remember. As time went on, not having to work on this day passed, but it has always been an easy day to remember.

It was a normal ceremony, but several strange things did happen. One was that my wife's youngest brother was only seven years old and he was crying his eyes out. He thought that when his sister was married, he would never see her again. She sat down with him and explained he was not losing a sister, but he was gaining a brother-in-law. At the reception, he came up to me and asked what it was like to have a seven-year-old brother-in-law. All was well. To this day, he is one of the only people I can remember his age, because I just do the math.

Another funny thing was my mother was a teetotaler, but my father did on occasion like to have a drink. She was watching him like a hawk, so he could not get anywhere near the bar at our wedding. She was right there if he did. Seeing his predicament, my cousin would buy a drink for my father and put it on top of the piano. Then he would go over to my father and say refreshments were on the key of C. From that day on, this was always an inside joke between my father and my cousin.

The minister came in sneakers, because after the wedding he had to judge the Fourth of July parade in town. We had to go to our motel after our marriage, but it was on the other side of a parade in Rockport, Massachusetts. I thought the best way to get to the motel was to become part of the parade. Well, it seemed that the nice policeman seeing my wife was in tears just asked me to park the car and walk the rest of the way, which fortunately was not very far. The next morning, the four little old ladies were having a great time in the room next to ours.

The first night of our honeymoon was in Rockport, but the next day, we flew across the pond to meet my wife's mother's side of the family and start our honeymoon in jolly old England. Even though Nova Scotia was my first time out of the country, I was really in a foreign country there. The cars were tiny and the roads were even smaller and you had to drive on the opposite side of the road. You constantly had to be reversing the way you think. Even walking around and stepping off a curb, you have to look right instead of left. I recently saw on TV that the heavily walked areas of London by Americans have a warning painted at the curb, "Look Right."

The dollar was stronger than the pound then and the whole honeymoon—flight, rental car, and a room at the airport when we arrived was $299 each. This also had included a cottage that was available, but we wanted to see as much of England as possible, so did not take advantage of that. After spending the first night at the airport to adjust for the jet lag, we head off to Windsor Castle on the way to Bath. We did all the tourist stuff; watching the changing of the guards and going to the Queen's state apartments and St. George's Cathedral along the way to Bath, named after the Roman Baths in the center of town.

We saw thatched cottages in the very picturesque town of Marlborough. I will never tire of these quaint cottages, but as the years go by and England comes into the twenty-first century, they are becoming scarcer because of several reasons. First, they are terrible fire hazards with a high insurance premium and have to be specially treated against such hazards. Secondly, the costs have gone out of sight and the tradesmen that have the knowledge and experience to install them are vanishing. The good point is they are said to last over one hundred years.

When we arrived at Bath, we stayed at the Northey Arms. That's another thing about England—the names of their pubs and inns. One of my favorite and fairly common names is the Spread Eagle Inn.

The Northey Arms had an excellent restaurant and pub. We had a very enjoyable evening settling into the old world. Some of the things we had to get used to even if we were speaking English was that there were different names for some things. Fags were cigarettes, a joint was a piece of meat, a biscuit was a cookie, and creamed potatoes were whipped. Give way meant yield, a roundabout was a rotary (they were really fun to get used to) and far more of them. A lay by was a rest area, a carriage way was a highway or road, a motorway was a turnpike, a lorry was a truck, and you did not pass a car—you overtook him.

A sign in Bath said, "Do not let your dog put a dirty mark in our park." These were just some of the expressions we found different. Another favorite was a banger—this was a sausage.

The English did not (contrary to popular belief) drink warm beer—it was cellar-chilled, meaning the kegs of beer were kept in the cooler cellars and pumped up to the bar. Another thing we had to get used to was you always said, "Cheers!" before each drink. It used to be very hard to get ice with a drink, but I'm told this is changing.

Back then the pubs closed at 10:30 p.m. and the smaller ones would close for lunch or supper, but you could get a pint or two and set on the steps and wait for them to reopen. When a pub was closing, they would call out, "Time, gentlemen, time," so you would know your time was up.

There is a legend that Bath was founded in 860 BC when Prince Bladud, father of King Lear, caught leprosy. He was banned from court and forced to look after the pigs. The pigs also had a skin disease, but after they wallowed in the hot mud, they were cured. Prince Bladud followed their example and was also cured. Later he became king and founded the city of Bath. This was a legend, but in reality, it is not known when the health-giving qualities of the Bath Springs were first noticed. The Romans have been dated to 50 AD and dedicated the Baths to Sul, a Celtic god and Minerva, the Roman god of healing. The Romans left England in 407 AD but the Baths are still there and a huge tourist trade still flourishes. On my way to the Baths, a local seeing that I was a tourist warned me not to drink the water. I believed he knew what he was talking about and took his advice.

After leaving Bath, we drove to Stonehenge, one of England's most famous landmarks. It is one of the most impressive places I have ever been. It is awe inspiring in its simplicity and antiquity. It is not known for sure exactly how old it is, but it is dated from about four to five thousand years old. Neolithic circles have just been found about two miles away from this area and are about ten thousand years old. When man went from food gatherers to food producers, as the glaciers receded, this discovery was on June 22, 2020. The mystery keeps growing, as the monoliths weighed up to four tons and were transported two hundred fifty miles from the Preseli Mountains in South Wales. The engineers of today do not know how it was done—possibly extraterrestrial visitors? Perhaps there is a connection to the Nan Madol culture, an island in Micronesia in the western Pacific Ocean, that scientists and engineers are still trying figure out how that site was built.

This is a place that should be visited by all tourists to England, but unfortunately it cannot be seen the way I saw it in 1970. I am told there is now a fence around it to keep vandals from defacing it. Like everywhere else, the crazy few have spoiled it for the 800,000 visitors a year. When I saw it, they had receded the car park across the street and when you walked through a tunnel under the road and came up, you basically saw a barren field with these eerie monoliths aligned to the celestial clock of the universe. There are many books written about this location and I highly recommend checking them out. My final word on the vandals is I hope England is not working up to the depravity of people wanting to tear down Lord Nelson's statue, because they do not like their country's history like here in the states.

Our next stop is Stratford-upon-Avon. A lot of English towns are quaint and beautiful, but Stratford abuses its privilege, having Shakespeare's birthplace, Anne Hathaway's cottage, and the Royal Shakespeare Globe Theater.

We strolled along the Avon River and had a drink at the Dirty Duck (another one of those cute names). Then we stayed at the Globe Hotel in Weedon, outside of Northampton.

From here we were off to Woburn Abby with a room decorated entirely with seashells and a Chinese room with two-hundred-year-old wallpaper. After a lunch of ox tail soup, we toured the game preserve—fortunately it was feeding time for lions, also. We gave the rhinos and giraffes the right of way, while the monkeys climbed on the bonnet, aka the hood of a car, and looked in at the monkey driving the car.

Then it was off to the Black Horse Pub to meet my wife's English family in Norwich, the city in which she was born during the war. When we get to the pub and walk in, a bunch of guys are standing at the bar. One of them says, "We think you are wanted on the other side." In England, there is a men's side and a family part of the bar. Even today, I think the tradition is fairly common for the entire family to go to a pub, rather than sitting around in a living room.

I have never felt more at home with any group as I did with her family. My wife's cousin, Philip, comes over to me and hands me a pint of beer and says, "This is your prayer book. There are 52 churches in Norwich, one for every week of the year, but 365 pubs, one for each day of the year."

Philip was in awe of my rental car. To me it was the smallest thing I had ever driven, but to Philip, it was the newest and biggest car he ever had a chance to drive. He asked me if he could take it for a spin. I could not see any harm and tossed him the keys. To this day, short of my ride in the 1963-427 HP Ford galaxy or my brother-in-law's son's 2018 Mustang with the 427 four-barrel and six-sped shift laying rubber in the first three gears out of the six, up to 130 MPH and hitting 160 on a county road in northern Ohio, it was the wildest ride in my life. Philip transformed into Sir Stirling Moss and my little rental Ford Cortina became his Maserati. I do have to say he made a good Stirling Moss, but who would have thought a Ford Cortina would have made a good Maserati?

To this day years later, I can say I have experienced something close to a grand Prix ride. When I got together with him a couple of years ago and reminded him of that ride, he was embarrassed that I had even remembered it.

In the room we were staying that night, I saw what I thought was some sort of antiquated water heater device. When you drew water, it heated it on demand. Now forty years later, this is state of the art in new homes today and regular water heaters are obsolete.

The next day we were off to see the city of Norwich, which included one of those 52 churches. The Norwich Cathedral dated back to 1100 AD. Coming from Boston, where one of the oldest houses is Paul Revere's, and the oldest church is the old North Church, which was Paul Revere's signal tower. 1100 years old makes these structures seem less impressive. Sorry, Boston historians, but I have to call it as it is. Everything is relative. Another stop was the Norwich castle museum that was built by the Romans as a Royal Palace nine hundred years ago.

The next place we went was Stranger's Hall, which stands on a foundation started in 1320 AD and has a considerable history in itself. The name of the hall remains a mystery though.

Much of the city is of flint, stone, and brick. At the end of the day, we went to the Blackhorse Pub and met my wife's great-aunt Millie, who was 88 years old and very sharp, so she had a right to her failing eyesight. We also met her Uncle Billie who had been tending his own pub called the Beaconsfield Pub.

The next day we tour the Norfolk coast on the North Sea, where years later we dispersed my mother-in-law's ashes, because she had played there as a child. We then returned to the Beaconsfield Pub and played a game of "niners." It was played on a board and was one of two left in all of England—quite an antique.

The following day we toured more of Norwich and visited Nurse Cavell's grave. (She was a Norwich World War I heroine, who was executed in Germany for aiding POWs.)

At the end of the day, we go to another of my wife's uncles for dinner. Uncle Fred and Aunt Ivy served a lovely dinner, and afterwards, we retire to the living room—the room my wife was born in. On the wall is a raised plate fifteen inches round of an English scene. When I compliment her on it, Ivy says, "You like it, take it. I am tired of it." This plate came home in my lap and now hangs on our bedroom wall. I have never tired of it.

Sadly, this house at 7 Drayton Road has seen the wrecking ball after surviving the German's bombings of World War II and, like a lot of places in our life, we cannot return to it.

Another gift he gave to us was a whiskey bottle that had ceramic tile glued to it and grouted. He also gave us a small bottle of mead. It is called a honeymoon drink, because it was supposed to be drank every night for the first month of the cycle of the moon and it consists of honey and wine. It also could have been honey and beer. The bottle was too small to have a drink from it for a whole month, but we kept it as a souvenir.

We also stopped at a pub that was managed by an elderly couple that had just got married. They were closing their pub and retiring, so they gave us a lot of stuff from the pub, so much that I thought we might have a problem coming back through customs. Some of the stuff they gave us were bar towels, optics, and pint mugs. The mugs had the Queen's measurements on them. A pint to the line or a pint to the brim. When you ordered a pint, it had to go either to the line or to the brim. The optics are used in some American bars, but English optics are controlled by a weight and measurement system of the government that give an exact gill and then it receives the queen's seal so you will get an exact pour—unlike a shot in the United States that is poured into a shot glass that could be a false pour by having a thick wall. This is why a bartender could give you a pour that looked like you were getting more, but you could still be getting screwed. With the Queen's optics and mugs, you are getting exactly what you have ordered.

When we left Norwich, I felt like I had gained a whole new family. Thinking about it, I really had, and a great one at that. As the years passed, they have come over here and we have gone over there and the bond has grown even more.

On Monday July 13th we head up to Edinburgh, Scotland. Arriving in the evening at 7:30 p.m., only to find our reservations had gone astray, but as luck would have it, we found a quaint old hotel in the Lamarka section of the city sitting on top of a hill and looking out over Edinburgh. Its name was the Glenburn and it was an old mansion that had been built in 1887 with a celestial observatory. I really felt at home.

We had a fantastic steak dinner in their dining room in the evening, then retired to our room at 11:00 p.m. to watch the sunset. Yes, Edinburgh is so far north that there is only about four hours of darkness in July. The next morning, we have a continental breakfast and the whole night's lodging with a private bath, dinner for two, and breakfast was only $27. Those were the days, as the song goes.

After breakfast, we head off to find Edinburgh Castle, which is immense and sits on a rocky elevation in the center of the city. However, we could not find it in the labyrinth of small streets and high buildings. We stop to ask for directions from some dust men, aka garbage men, all dressed in shirt and ties with tweed sports coats and very friendly. After having a very interesting conversation, which we really could understand, in a thick Scottish accent, they gave us very clear directions to the castle.

When we arrive at the castle, we find it is in the throes of preparing for the Royal Tattoo, which is billed as one of the world's most spectacular events with two hundred fifty of the finest pipers and drummers. It's held every August and has to be booked two years in advance.

Sadly, we will miss it, because we have a date with Nessie in northern Scotland. Also we do not have the reservations needed for any of the events and must be home in less than a week. We return to our hotel and have another fantastic supper. We leave bright and early to catch a glimpse of the strange beast that draws tourists into this remote and beautiful land. The Scots are not dumb people. Nothing short of a strange elusive creature in a remote loch could draw tourists north of Edinburgh. I have to admit the area is hauntingly beautiful—even if Nessie did stand us up.

After spending a day checking every ripple in Loch Ness, we come to Blair Castle, which was once the home of the Duke of Athall. It was every bit a perfect example of a storybook castle, in white stucco instead of the customary stone.

I never found Nessie, but I did spend the day dodging sheep in the middle of nowhere. We finally run across Urquhart Castle, another castle that was classic, but in timeless ruin. When I returned years later, it was still in ruin, but the landscaping was outstanding.

At the end of the day, we arrive in Fort Augustus and rented a room in the Lovat Hotel. I do not think there was any connection to Lyle.

The room required a shilling to start the heater and there was the bedpan, aka thunder jug, in the closet—not the jug from Robert Mitchum's song (*Thunder Road*). After we enter our room, I look out our window and see a mast of a sailboat drifting past. This to me was really strange, so I go down to investigate. I find a canal going through the town to enter into Loch Ness. It seems this bypassed all of northern Scotland to get to the North Sea.

That evening during supper, we order a pack lunch for the next day. After breakfast, we head south along Loch Lomond and its Norwegian style fjords and the cloud-covered barren mountains. Then, as the song goes, we have our box lunch on the shore of Loch Lomond. Not a fancy ham sandwich, but crisps, aka potato chips, an apple, cake, biscuits, and cheese. We remain totally unaware of our future mechanical problems.

We drive through Glasgow and I apologize for not being able to say anything nice about this city. Only if Scotland ever needed an enema, this is where they would insert the tube. I think this says it all and I give credit to Chris Wallace's *Countdown 1945* of the impression of Wendover, Utah.

About thirty miles south of Glasgow, my Ford Cortina, aka Maserati, died. It might have something to do with how Sir Stirling Moss had handled it.

As we sit there in the middle of nowhere, I said to my bride, "I will go get help. There has to be a pub nearby." Lo and behold, in keeping with the true nature of the British Isles, I walk across a field next to the car and behold, there sits a pub. I call Avis Car Rental and they say they will have a car out in less than an hour. They show up with a tow truck and a new car and we are off.

Thanks to a Scottish policeman and a AA man, aka AAA man, we reach Carlisle. They say we would have a better chance in Perth, where we found an RAC serviceman, who took us in because they had run a bed and breakfast at their house. He left a note for his wife that we were in the guest bedroom.

The next morning when we came down, she had a fantastic breakfast all set up for us on their patio. The fee was two pounds or about five dollars. After a lovely chat with the wife, we're off to London. We arrive about 5 p.m. and find a room in Greenwich called The Regency. Unfortunately, the food did not live up to its name, but one bad meal out of fourteen is not bad.

Being a boater, I find the clipper ship, the Cutty Sark, that brought tea back from China. The first clipper back would put a piece of hemp rope in the hand of the figurehead, which was wearing a flimsy nightgown, aka a Cutty Sark. The legend goes that Farmer Tam encounters a coven of witches, including beautiful witch Nannie, wearing a Cutty Sark. She spots Tam spying on them and peruses him on his horse, Maggie. He knows if he passes over water, the witch cannot follow. However, she grabs a piece of Maggie's tail as Tam escapes. The Scottish definition of Cutty means short and Sark is a form of nightgown.

The other vessel that was next to the Cutty Sark was the Gypsy Moth IV. This was Sir Frances Chichester's vessel that he singled-handedly went around the world in at age 65. I have read that they have moved her to Buckler Hard in Hampshire. For his accomplishment, the Queen knighted him.

Here I have to mention Joshua Slocum, an eccentric sea captain out of Fairhaven, Massachusetts. He has had several books written about him, the best being *A Man for All Oceans,* by Stan Grayson. Joshua was lost at sea going to South America on or after November 14, 1909. My one and only my thought is that he took a knock down off Cape Hatteras only because I took one at the same time of year without any bad weather around. They say he was spotted off Venezuela, but nothing is positive, except that he never made it back. I only mention him, because my sailing days covered all the places in the book and he was legendary in New England.

Another single-hander is Dodge Morgan. He was bigger than life and an acquaintance of mine from the power squadron. He was a newspaper publisher from Maine who sailed the American Promise around the world without touching land. He originally left Marblehead, Massachusetts, but he experienced electrical problems and dropped in to Bermuda to correct them. His around-the-world trip started and ended with Bermuda. His trip was 27,000 miles and he did it in 150 days. He told me he thought the tough part was going to be physical, but it turned out to be mental, with the mind thinking strange things. The vessel cost 1.5 million and was built by C. W. Hood Yachts. His trip was from 1985 through 1986. It was a sixty-foot sloop with all the bells and whistles.

When he got back, he gave the Promise to the Naval Academy with the stipulation it could not be sold, so nobody could buy it and beat his record. The Naval Academy cadets proceeded to cut off a barge in the Chesapeake and sank it, but they raised it. When he went to the academy, the commodore asked if he wanted to see it. His reply was that he could not go to the love of his life, which had been raped by his cadets. This part of the story is second-hand, but I have enough faith in my source to repeat it. Dodge died on September 17, 2010. Another great sailor has gone in search of the green flash.

I checked and quite a few people have circumnavigated the world. I think a couple have beaten Dodge's record. I know a few were multi-hulls, which is like the Ford Cortina and the Maserati. However, they cannot compare to a sloop. It is like the America's Cup—it is all different. Yes, they are sailboats, but it all went south with the wing keel. I have sailed a wing and they are faster, but as a purest, they should be different classes.

Another famous feature of Greenwich is the Greenwich Meridian, from which all navigational calculations are derived. At this spot, my wife asks what time is it. My reply was, "Greenwich Mean Time."

We settle in for the evening and get up early to drive to Parliament Square, home of Big Ben. At last we had found the London we imagined and had coffee and pastry. We walk about three miles to the tower of London. It was a pleasant stroll with parks, bums, and the inevitable pigeons—a typical big city, but the tower was unique with the most extensive collection of suits of armor ever assembled, along with the crown jewels, diamonds, emeralds, and rubies, along with more solid gold than you could imagine. Most incredible was the vault—foolproof, and if a movie could be made of cracking of its security system, it would be a thriller.

One thing that stands out in my mind even today was that you had to keep moving. You could not stand there to look at anything. I could tell that this was part of the security system with the surreptitious coverage, along with yeoman wardens and guards around the tower. For atmosphere there were the ravens whom legend foretells, if they leave the tower, England will fall.

Ravens are incredible birds of great mystery and held in high esteem in English legend. The native American Indians felt the same toward them. There are books written about this playful mystical bird. Some of them are *Mind of the Raven* by Bernd Heinrich, *Mark of the Raven* by Morgan Busse, *Day of the Raven* by Michell Jon MacKay, *In the Shadow of the Raven* by Joseph Vargo and William Piotrowski, and two others by Edgar Allen Poe: *Petersburg: The Untold Story of the Raven* and *The Raven*.

From the Tower of London, we did what every tourist should do and took a taxi to Oxford Street, the main shopping district of London, where we passed Trafalgar Square and Lord Nelson on his pedestal. Working in retail all my life, I was overwhelmed by the department store—Selfridges with 540,000 square feet of sales floor, second largest in England, with Harrods being the largest. My wife bought our china service (Royal Dalton's Berkshire pattern) and I got my pigskin English dartboard, which we brought back with us. However, the china service took four months to receive due to a dock strike. It seems whenever we go to Europe, there is a strike. Most of them are only for a few days, but some can be considerably longer.

Realizing our time in England is almost over and there are still places we want to see, we take a taxi back to Parliament Square for a tour of the House of Commons and House of Lords. Next we head for one of the most impressive castles in the world, Dover Castle. It's situated on the White Cliffs of Dover, facing England's most formidable foe—at least back in castle time.

Castle time was over a fairly long period in Europe, but a short time in the United States. In Europe, the weaponry was crossbows and catapults, whereas in the United States, it was rifles and cannons. In Europe, castles are everywhere from the medieval times. In the United States, they are on the harbor of every major city on the East Coast.

There are two major castles in Boston—one on the outer harbor on Georges Island, Fort Warren, and one on the inner harbor on Castle Island, Fort Independence. These two forts were called the knuckles of Boston and made it very protected.

Fort Sumter is in Charleston Harbor, which is where the Civil War started. Fort McKinley is where the *Star Spangled Banner* was written in Baltimore. Other forts not so famous were Fort Amsterdam and Fort George in New York at the tip of Manhattan and Fort Norfolk in Norfolk, Virginia. All these forts have had books written about them, although very few saw any action for which they were designed.

The prisoners could write to their wives uncensored. One of the prisoners wrote to his wife with explicit detailed directions on how to free him, giving his cell location and the time of a new moon when it would be the darkest. His directions were to steal a rowboat in Hull and row over to the fort and free him. On the night of the new moon, his wife following his instructions, gets on the island. A guard detects her movement and commands her to halt. Not heeding the command, he shoots and finds he has killed a lady all dressed in black. To this day the ghost of the lady in black still walks the ramparts of Georges Island on eerie dark nights of a new moon.

Years ago, I sailed to this fort and found a chalk drawing of the lady in black and Captain Warren, the man the fort was named after.

This drawing had been done by Sidewalk Sam, a famous street artist of Boston. I have digressed Big time. Back to Dover, England.

Meanwhile, heading south, we come across Broome Park Hotel. I leave my bride in the car and walk into the Twilight Zone and what appeared to be the great hall to a castle. At one end was a massive snooker table, I would say was ten by twenty feet. At the other end was a medieval dining room table about forty feet long with chairs all around it. Next to the table was a small desk. The man sitting there could have been a double for Lurch of the TV show, *The Adams Family*. I asked if he had a room and he said yes and he would show it to me.

We walk to the other end of the great hall and went up the huge staircase. Climbing the stairs, I cannot help but notice the gargoyles staring at me on every post of the bannister. When we arrive at the hallway on the second floor, I notice that all the pictures on the wall are of people being tortured or dismembered. Being in the middle of nowhere, I reluctantly register and return for my bride. I tell her that we have a lovely room with a private bath and yes, a very good lock on the door. I thought our host was most gracious, but so was Count Dracula. It is very hard to explain how strange this place was. It has to be one of the strangest places I have ever stayed.

Some of the reasons to back up my feelings was that night was the first night I heard the cry of the raven in England. It is similar to a crow but with caw, caw-caw, whereas, a crow is caw-caw. The next thing is that I have to take honeymoon pictures to remember (Hotel Strange). When I return home, all my pictures came out perfect. Yes, all but Broome Park—a blank roll. How strange is that!!!

Seven years later, I return to get a room there. They said that they were a Riding Academy and it had never been a hotel!!! That night we drove down the road a couple of miles for a drink and a snack at the Jackdaw Pub. We had a nice conversation with the bartender and fended off a massive white cat that thought our meal was really his. The locals thought this quite humorous. On our way back to Broome Park, it was the only time I slipped up by driving on the wrong side of the road. Wondering why that car was coming at me, I quickly came to my senses and got back on the right side of the road. After two drinks, you let your guard down when having to stay on the left. The next morning, we go to the dining room, which is separate from the great hall. After not seeing another person in this Twilight Zone, the dining hall is full of people.

After breakfast we head off to Dover Castle, which is the largest in England. Originally this site may have been fortified with earth works before the Romans invaded in 43 AD. But the fort as it appears today was rebuilt in the twelfth century. In true keeping with England's damp, wet weather, we spend our last day absorbing the ancient atmosphere and what England is all about—history.

While in England, I learned some strange sayings and old English anecdotes.

June was the month of choice for weddings, because people took their yearly bath in May. But starting to smell in June, brides would carry a bouquet of flowers to hide any body odor. Hence the tradition of carrying a bouquet when getting married.

When it came to baths, the man of the house used the clean water first. He was followed by the sons, then the women, and lastly the children, and finally the baby. Hence the saying, "Don't throw the baby out with the bath water."

The cats and dogs would get warm by hiding in the thatched

roofs. When it rained, it would get slippery and sometimes, they would fall off. Hence, the expression, "Raining cats and dogs."

Other little creatures would live in the thatch and fall onto the beds, so people would put up posts and stretch sheets over them to stop those unpleasant visitors. Thus, the creation of the canopy bed.

Only the rich could afford tiled floors. The floors of the poor were dirt. Thus, dirt poor. These dirt floors got slippery when it rained, so they would spread thresh or straw to help keep their footing. As time wore on, the thresh would build up, so they would put a board in the entrance way, which became the "threshold."

Cooking in those days was done in a big kettle that hung over a fire and the kettle was just left hanging there. Leftovers were added each day, being basically of vegetables. For quite a while, it was the foundation of the rhyme: peas porridge hot, peas porridge cold, peas porridge in the pot nine days old.

Sometimes they could obtain pork, so they're bringing home the bacon. Then they would share it. Thus, chewing the fat.

The rich had plates made out of pewter and food with a high acid content caused some of the lead to leach into the food, causing lead poisoning. This was very common with tomatoes. For four hundred years, tomatoes were considered poisonous in England and to this day still are called, "uglies."

Another strange custom was with bread. Workers got the burnt bottom, the family got the middle, and the guest got the top or upper crust.

Excessive ale or whiskey was drunk out of lead cups and would knock the imbiber out for a couple of days. They would lay them out for a couple of days on the kitchen table and every one would gather around and eat and drink and wait to see if they would awake. Hence, the custom of holding a wake.

Another strange thing about a burial was that they would reuse the graves, because of lack of space in the church graveyards. When the coffins were raised, about one out of twenty-five would have scratch marks on the inside. They realized that they had been burying people alive. So someone got the brilliant idea to tie a string around the corpse's wrist. They ran the string up to the surface and tie a bell to it. Hence, he sat out the graveyard shift. If the person was alive, he was saved by the bell or he was a dead ringer. Yes, the other saved by the bell was a fighter taking the ten count after being knocked down and the bell ringing before the count was finished. The bell at the grave was eliminated, when the mortician embalmed the corpse.

Another old English legend is that of the rhyme, *Ring around the Rosie*. People have associated that with the great plague of 1665 or earlier outbreaks of the black death of the 1340s. A rosy rash was a symptom of the plaque. Posies or herbs were carried as protection to ward off or cover up the smell. Ashes, ashes refers to the cremation of the bodies or burning the victim's house to help kill the evil spirts. All fall down is what the victims did at the time of their demise. I always thought this was a strange children's poem or song. The strangest thing of all is that there are people who think the plague of 1665, 1340, and most recently, COVID 19 have arrived from meteors carrying bacteria from outer space, because it has been proven that it can survive extreme cold.

CHAPTER 11

Coming Home

Arriving back at Heathrow, I can tell we are back in the twentieth century sitting on the runway looking out at Concord Jet that can cross the Atlantic in three and a half hours and fast forwarding forty years to my landing at de Gaulle Airport in the twenty-first century and seeing possibly the same Concord Jet mounted on a pedestal as a memory of the past. How strange is that? How time does fly. No pun intended!!

When we get back to our apartment, we find our bathroom has been stuffed with a year's supply of newspaper, because we left the keys with our friends to bring our wedding gifts back. One of our friends lived upstairs, so we had to use their bathroom for three days until we finally got it emptied. They did feel sorry for us when they saw how tired we were and told us about the alarm clock they had hidden under our bed to go off in the middle of the night.

Returning to everyday life in the retail world part of my daily duties was vacuuming and dusting the furniture department in which I worked. One day I noticed a stain on our best king mattress displayed in the bedding aisle and I bring it to the attention of my boss. Back then you could flip a mattress periodically, so he said we will just flip it. A couple of weeks later, the stain is back on the turned side. With the stain being questionable, we have to order a new mattress and again a couple of weeks later, a new stain appears. After establishing that the roof is not leaking, this recurring stain becomes a serious issue and security is called in on the mystery. One day I am doing my routine vacuuming, when the vacuum hits something under the bed. The mystery is solved. I find a wallet belonging to the boss of the cleaning crew that came in twice a week. It seems in his pleasure on our best bed, he had taken his wallet out of his pocket and put it under the bed, but forgot about it. Like the dumb thief that holds up a bank with the note written on his deposit slip, we had the culprit with the "DNA," even though that was not heard of back then, but the wallet was just as good.

During this time, security was becoming a little more sophisticated. I say that, because some of the old ways to catch a thief were kind of primitive. Like the time a cashier was suspected of borrowing money without asking or returning it. This is my way of being nice and not calling the person an out-and-out thief. They cut a hole through the manager's office wall and laid planks or boards on the suspended ceiling over to the cashier's office and installed what looked like a vent in the ceiling. Security would crawl out on his stomach and lay there for hours and watch the suspect. The funny part of this whole process was that as time went by, the suspended ceiling began to sag—why it never collapsed no one will ever know. However, they did catch the thief.

As we started to modernize with security cameras, the automotive department thought it entertaining to moon the cameras before the store opened. It did not take long before the cameras were stolen and had to be more securely replaced.

The automotive section was a separate building, as were most of

Sears automotive departments, because the mechanics would track in the oil and grease into the main store. There were exceptions to this rule, but not many.

There was a customer who would come in and help the guys in a snowstorm move tires up from the basement, which was as large as the bay area. How this started I do not know. The man was a funeral director and he stopped showing up for about three months. When he finally came back in, he said he had almost died handling what he called a hot body.

In later years after I had left Sears, a fellow that I had known and could have ended up being my boss came to talk to me. He said I should close out my profit-sharing and invest in the company for which he now worked, because Sears was not doing well. I kind of had that feeling and felt he was right. Hind sight showed that I doubled my investments with him, but I would have lost a lot if I had stayed with Sears. I went with his company and we would meet once a year and go over my account, which took about an hour. Twenty minutes would be for my account. Another twenty would be for boating, because we were both boaters. the final twenty minutes would be for Sears stories that he could not talk to me about when we both worked there.

One of his stories was about a fellow I knew and heard stories about him being a tyrant. This person held a meeting every Monday with his staff and trainees. All the people in the meeting were men, except for one quiet and diligent female trainee. While he was on his weekly rant, she simply sat listening while she crocheted. This drove him crazy—he didn't have to go too far. He crept up behind her and stood there for a couple of minutes. When she finally looked around, he said, "You must really enjoy crocheting—it must be like masturbating."

She simply said, "When I crochet, I crochet. When I masturbate, I masturbate!!"

She shot him out of the sky—this could not happen today. This was thirty years ago.

CHAPTER 12

Jack

My friend, Jack, had returned from Vietnam and said he had a friend who was selling a sailboat for $5,000. We decided to go look at it in Mattapoisett, Massachusetts, and decided $2,500 each was not bad. The rest is history. The owner had told Jack it had been sunk in a hurricane and the engine had been pulled, rebuilt, and was setting under the boat. We told him if he could get it running, we would buy it. And he did. And we did.

Our first business was a name for our craft. Its old name meant seasick in French. This had to be agreed upon by his wife and mine and by him and me. However, a committee of four is tough to come to an agreement on anything—a name is particularly hard.

When I went into work, I mentioned our problem. A fellow I worked with said, "Try Halcyon." He said to look it up in the

dictionary. It had two meanings. The first was a bird of the ancients that nested on the waters and calmed everyone. The modern meaning was a derivate meaning calm and peaceful, so halcyon it was. Quite frequently it refers to a period of your life, calm and peaceful in life's journey. These were definitely mine, as I tear up.

The partnership worked well, because Jack was off on Saturday and I was off on Wednesday and he had it one Sunday and I had it the next Sunday, while the third Sunday we went out together. All expenses were split 50/50 and, in the winter, Jack worked on the boat on Saturday and I worked on it on Wednesday and we went up on every Sunday together. His talents were more mechanical and mine were more paint and powder or in the boating world, marine tech to fill in the holes.

One Sunday we would bring a six pack of beer and the next Sunday, a bottle of wine. We always knocked off around 2:00 p.m.to walk around the marina to socialize. This is what winter boating is all about. One Sunday, we got our wires crossed and we ended up with wine and beer. This was not good and we did not have the brains to drink only one of the selections. After our socializing, we realized we needed food. Jack was not a very big guy, but his ability to consume an 18-ounce steak was amazing. When we stopped at our favorite restaurant, the waitress said it would be a few minutes before we could be seated, so if we go to the bar and have a drink, she would call us when she had a table. This was not the best idea, but a scotch did sound pretty good.

This restaurant was on a pond and had two floating gazebos, one attached to the next with a little bridge. After we had a huge meal, the first gazebo was generally used for people to have an after-dinner drink and watch the ducks, geese, and swans swimming around. The second gazebo was the sanctum-sanctorum for lovers. After dinner, I tell Jack I am going to the men's room.

When I come out, I can't find him, so I go out to the first gazebo—no Jack! I look out to the second gazebo and see him close to a couple. The guy was on bended knee with a small box in hand. Jack in close proximity is leaning over the rail. How should I put this nicely? He was feeding the water fowl a hot meal that had recently been enjoyed by Jack. Jack is no longer with us, but in his defense, it was the only time I ever saw him get sick. He always cringed when I told this story, but I have a sick sense of humor and I had to tell it again. I often wonder how that poor couple is doing today, after such a strange start.

At this time, I have to tell you Jack's favorite line. "Let's get together and swap stories and tell lies with an adult beverage." Not necessarily in that order.

Jack was the engine maintenance man and I was the painter. One day he is in the engine room for what I thought was quite a long time, so I peek in and ask him how it was going. It seems the only way to drain the oil was this little pump with a throw on its handle of about a quarter to a half an inch. His reply was memorable: "It was like jerking off a mouse." I'm not sure how he knew what that was like.

In the spring we were sailing down from winter storage in Great Bay by Portsmouth, New Hampshire, and going to Marblehead where a storm was moving in from sea. Normally we would go through the Annisquam River, but Jack had concerns about the fan belt and thought we should sail around Cape Ann. As night engulfed us with lightning and heavy rain, my concern was being too close to Thatcher Island. Every time the lightning flashed, it looked like we were being blown into Thatcher's rocks with the waves breaking over them. It was really just the white caps of the storm, but I have to say this was one of the most uncomfortable nights I have ever spent on a night passage—not only were we wet, but I was really cold.

As morning came, I thought of the song, "There has to be a morning after." The storm had abated and now we are becalmed and out of sight of land. Jack wants to save our fan belt for negotiating the tight passage through Marblehead Harbor, so being totally frustrated, he climbs into the dingy and ties a line to the bow of the boat and stern of the dingy and starts to row in. Fortunately, the wind picks up in about half an hour and I get Jack back in the boat, so we sail into Marble with dignity, like nothing had happened. This was one of Jack's traits. He could not just sit there and wait for the wind to pick up. He always had to be doing something to feel he was in control, no matter how slight.

Having kept the Halcyon in Boston the first year, Jack asked me if I would like to keep it in Marblehead the next year. Bear in mind, the people of Marblehead believe their town is the sailing capital of the world. They might not be too far off, but I have been in a lot of harbors that felt the same way. The interesting part of this offer was there would be no cost. Boston was expensive, so I asked him what was the catch. He said a friend of his had sold his boat and did not have one at this time. If he did not keep a boat on the mooring, he would lose the mooring. Jack and Bill came up with a solution. We make Bill a third partner, so he could keep the mooring and he would have a boat to go and sit on and have a beer in the evening.

The only problem to this solution was parking. The town had a field that you could park in, which worked the first year. The second year, the town allowed a supermarket and strip mall to be built on this space. Then we had to go a little further away and park in a school lot that summer, which worked out fairly well, too.

On the Fourth of July, we came down to watch the fireworks over the harbor, which were spectacular, followed by an illumination around the harbor shoreline that was made up of candles in paper bags every ten feet.

We spend the night on the boat and go into a popular breakfast shop in the morning. There is a small line, but we got seated quickly at a table for four. As we sit down, Jack remembers that he forgot something on the boat and says he will be right back. Shortly after Jack is gone, a guy comes over and asks if he could sit with us. I said no, somebody was with us and he went back out to the boat to get something, but that he would be right back. He asks if we had a boat in the harbor and I said yes. He then asked for the name of the boat and not thinking, I told him and he left in a funk.

The next time we came back to the boat we found we had been cited with three false violations. It seems the arrogant guy in the breakfast shop was the assistant harbor master. It took a day out of my life to resolve these bogus violations. I will say no more. Fortunately, this was the last year with the Halcyon and we sold it that winter. We sold it for what we paid for it and never saw it again.

Bill, our third partner, bought the ugliest barge he could find to put on the mooring. I bought a Catalina 30 and Jack started a computer supply company.

I went back to Boston and got my captain's license and spent another twenty years in Boston with Sail Boston booking my charters. I stayed with Sears, but the charters were a side event with a lot of flexibility to take people out when Sail Boston needed me.

One day I'm out with friends in Salem Harbor at Great Misery Island (named from a fire at a hotel on the island) The hotel had a golf course and during prohibition a bar. It seemed it was a hard place to raid, because they could see the authorities coming on a liquor raid. While sitting in the cockpit with my friends, one person said, "My God, what an ugly boat!" Lo and behold, it was my friend and past partner of the Halcyon, "Bill." He comes over to say hi, much to the embarrassment of my guest.

Throughout the years, a lot of Jack's friends became mine. Two interesting stories come to mind. The first story was about Roger, who had gone to college with Jack's wife, while Jack was in Vietnam. When he returned, Roger and his wife became friends with Jack. In the summer, Roger drove a taxi in New York City and lived in New Jersey on the other side of the Hudson River.

When Jack asks if I would like to go see a play in New York and visit Roger and his wife, I said yes. It is interesting to go to New York City with someone that knows the city. I should qualify this story and I don't know if it is this bad now, but when we got out of the play and are walking back to the car, it seems we had about ten thugs fallowing us. I had not noticed this till Roger leaned over to me and said, "As soon as I tell you, grab Ginny and cross the street." He then tells Jack the same. It seems he heard the thugs picking out who was going to jump who. Roger, having worked in New York, knew if we crossed the street, we were out of their hood, and they could not go into another gang's territory or "hood."

We then went to an ice cream parlor, which smelled like a grow house. We bought some ice cream and went back to his house to relax.

A couple of years later, I get a call from Jack asking if I would like to help Roger out with a business problem. I said yes and he gave me Roger's phone number. It seems he was working in the Midwest for a meat distributor and some bad chicken had been shipped to local fast-food restaurants and supply houses in New England with salmonella. At least, they thought the chicken had salmonella and had to be picked up without the news media getting wind of it. Then they would put it on dry ice to be shipped back to be tested. I worked out what I thought was a fair price for this clandestine recovery of bad chicken. I will not go into the names of the places I went, but the one memorable stop was a meat packing processing plant in Boston. If you like hot dogs, you might not want to read the next paragraph.

I walk into the room looking for who is in charge. There I find the workers playing catch with a bull's penis before it went into the hotdog vat. It looked like a basketball player scoring the winning point for the Celtics.

I didn't see Roger often in my retirement in Florida. However, one time when I brought my trawler to Sanford down the St. Johns River, I get a call from Jack. He said he was also coming to visit with him and it seems he is only a couple of miles from where I am keeping the boat. He asks me if I would like to go visit Roger. My reply was, "Does a bear do poopy in the woods?" We make arrangements to meet and go to Roger's gated community together.

After visiting Roger for a while, he asks if we would like to see the rest of the complex. We say yes and take off in his golf cart to a second gate in his community. Passing through this gate, I realize most of the houses in this area are mansions with their own gates. As I have said before, I know I have led a simple life, but I didn't know that there were people living in triple-gated communities.

When we get back to Roger's house, we go upstairs to his office. There he shows us what he does now with his computer—he tracks over sixty to seventy trucks and controls the delivery of perishable flowers all over the East Coast. He tracks the speed of the trucks, checks to see if the drivers are getting their required rest, and if they are on schedule.

When Jack and I first bought Halcyon, we were aware of the fact that our nautical knowledge was lacking. We decided a boating class would help out, even though I had lived by the water all my life. We took a basic boating course with the Power Squadron, which is an organization that nationally teaches safe boating courses. As time goes on, Jack got tied up getting his computer supply company up and running and I got involved in the many Power Squadron courses that are available.

CHAPTER 13

Power Squadron

I started teaching some of the classes and like most organizations, leadership was needed, so I got talked into helping in that capacity. (as a side note, I have found this is the way it happens with most organizations.)

These classes became very interesting and the basis of many long-lasting friendships. One of the more interesting people I met—and as I say there were many—was a retired doctor that lived in an old Victorian mansion built by a retired civil war general. It was next door to another house built by the general's brother. This house had been bought by his father, who was also a doctor. He had taken the stables on the next street and made them into a hospital.

As the years passed, we would get tours of the house, aka mansion, basically because of things Doc wanted to show us. Doc had been building a sailboat in his backyard and he brings us out to see it. While he is showing us this 42-foot craft made of mahogany, one of the other fellows who was a carpenter leans over to me and whispers, "What do you think of the sheer?"

Even I could see it was off by seven inches and though it looked lovely, it could never sail. This was not a problem, because Doc was around eighty years old. The boat had given him something do in his senior years. After he died, I think the boat also went to boat heaven.

Doc wanted to show us the winches he was making in the cellar. As we are walking toward his shop in the basement, I can't help but notice a fifteen-foot train switching engine, so I had to ask what it was doing in the basement.

To him, the answer was simple. During the depression the boiler had failed and his father could not find one large enough to heat the house. However, he did know somebody who worked for the B&M Railroad, who just happened to have a spare switching engine laying around. The driveway went down a hill, so the wall could be knocked out and Wa-La—a new heating system. Yes, it all seemed so simple to Doc, having lived with it all his life.

All the sheets for the hospital were washed in a machine that had come off a submarine. In the foyer was a large staircase and on the first post of the banister stood a miniature suit of armor about two feet tall. When you lifted the visor, it lit up the entire staircase.

Throughout the house were old oil lamps on the walls that had been wired for electric lights. On the third floor was a full ballroom.

It was very much like the grandeur of the Webb estate I had known as a child.

Another person that I had become friendly with was George C. Scott—not the famous actor/war hero, but just as interesting a person. He was still racing in the Head of the Charles scull races at eighty. His house was in Essex, Massachusetts, on the Ipswich River, with seventy acres of land. Being in the heating business with Sears, I found his heating system very interesting. The furnace could be fired with coal, wood, or oil. The house originally sat only feet from the Ipswich River and flooding had always been a problem, so he had it moved to the top of the hill. I was told that his family had made out very well in the electric plating business, but he was very frugal—and proud of his Chevy Corvair—not Corvette.

After losing his first wife when he came to my house for Power Squadron meetings or parties, he would always come early to go upstairs to visit my mother-in-law, who lived with us. She used to complain that I never introduced her to any wealthy old men. I told her I didn't want to hear about it, because George was wealthy and interested.

George was the only person I knew that had a pig roast on his 80th birthday party. The pig caught fire and the flames were twenty feet high. Somebody grabbed a hose and when the pig was finally extinguished, they wanted to throw him out. Cooler heads prevailed—no pun intended, so when the piggy cooled down, we cut him open—he was delicious.

George told us his son was a fisherman in Alaska. During the Exxon Valadez oil spill, he brought out the news reporters for $700 a day, instead of fishing.

Sadly, George came to a strange and untimely end. His brother lived in Denver, Colorado, and when he died, George (not wanting to fly) takes off to Colorado in his beloved Corvair in the middle of winter. Two days into his trip, he slides off the road and the car can't be fixed quickly, so he gets to a dealer and writes a check for another Corvair and continues on. The next day his second car slides off the road and is totaled, so he gets a ride to the closest dealer. There he again writes a check and gets another Corvair and continues on. In the twenty years I knew George, he never wore a coat or jacket in the winter. He only wore a red plaid wool shirt. Finally, close to Denver, he gets lost in a snowstorm and ends up off the main road and slides into a ditch. They found his frozen body, which indicated that he had tried to walk back to the main road. As time went on, they traced his travels by his cancelled checks and talking to the dealerships from whom he had purchased his cars. This is how they figured out his sad demise.

Probably the most vivacious person I ever knew was a member of our squadron and the lawyer for Georgetown, Massachusetts. We needed a guest speaker for one of our dinners, so Bob volunteered to speak on off-shore sailing and moving yachts for Caribbean yacht charters.

When he was finished, I went up to him and told him if he ever needed help and another crew member, I would love to help. About six months later, he calls me up and asks if I was serious about my offer. and I said, yes.

The owner of Caribbean Yacht Charters (CYC) used Bob a lot to move boats, because he had an office and staff that could handle almost anything, so his time was pretty much his own, and he loved sailing. CYC had a new Hylas 49 hull, #1 in the Annapolis boat show that had to be delivered to St. Thomas. Bob puts together a crew of six of us and I tell him I have a brother-in-law who lives in the Annapolis area who can help us provision the boat for the two-week trip.

We get the boat provisioned and then have a laundry list of things that have to be checked out for its maiden voyage. The yacht was made in mainland China and I believed it made a west coast port of entry and was hauled across country. (One story that goes with this type of operation is about a boat being hauled over the Rockies. When they stopped overnight in freezing weather, the block froze, because it had not been winterized.)

Bob sets up a watch system of two-hours for each person. Two hours watching for debris and keeping the helms person company, two hours on the helm, and eight hours for rest and refreshment. This gave two twelve-hour cycles for twenty-four hours. Finally, we are off and going down the Chesapeake with which none of us are familiar. During the day is easy, as we just follow the sea buoys for the freighters and tankers going to Baltimore, Maryland. For people that are not familiar with the difference, it is simple—tankers carry fuel and freighters carry freight. It's that simple. The problem comes with the freight, because most of it is in containers. Even though they are tied strapped down, occasionally the straps fail and the containers get washed off. When this happens, in most cases, they do not sink. Their buoyancy is such that they float just under the surface a foot or two or on the surface. Quite a few boats have sunk when they hit these nautical hazards. This was not a problem in the Chesapeake, but what we were not aware of was only every other buoy was lit. As we are moving along at about ten knots, I catch something out of the corner of my eye about two feet from the boat. It was an unlit sea buoy. These things are huge. We were very lucky and get out the charts to see only every other one is lit. I tell this story to my brother-in-law and he says all the locals are aware this and tell him all of Boston's sea buoys are lit.

We finally make it out into open waters and head south into the unknown and the Bermuda Triangle. As day turns into night, it is my turn at the helm and yes, we all had safety harnesses on. As night came, the sea was building, but not "really" bad for a 49-foot sailboat. I learned that waves can get out of sync and build with one another and the next thing you know, you have what is called a rogue wave, which hit us in the Bermuda Triangle. If we had been in a smaller boat or not sealed up with all the hatches closed and dorade boxes sealed and ports closed, I would not be here now. I had just taken the helm and not secured my safety harness, when I hear this breaking wave over my left shoulder. I glimpsed back to see about a thirty-foot wave breaking over us. I grab the wheel as tightly as I could and take a breath of air, because I knew I was going to be underwater for a while. It seemed like a minute, but it was probably only forty seconds. The wave filled the sail and carried the mast into the water, but the boat continued to move forward. Eventually, the force was so great, I was washed to the rear stanchions. My watch partner, who was the only female on board, was washed to the starboard stanchions and caught there. Because of the weight in the keel, the boat finally popped upright and the wave was gone. Clair was still wrapped around the starboard stanchions.

This area is off Cape Hatteras and in the Bermuda Triangle. When Joshua Slocum vanished in the spray in 1909, they had ruled out a rogue wave, because there had been no storms in the area. We had not had a storm either and our boat was bigger and in better shape. However, we learned that storms are not a prerequisite for rouge waves. Joshua was spotted off Trinidad, but that was only a rumor. I now believe this is the fate of a lot of missing boats. We were just lucky. The rogue wave story was told to my mother on the night Paul washed the sail.

You might be wondering about the World War II fighters, Flight 19 on December 5, 1945, that flew into this area and disappeared. In this case, the magnetic field is really screwy and does not go north and south—I believe it even fluctuates. They thought their compasses were malfunctioning, but compasses don't really malfunction—they can have deviation, which is not really a malfunction.

After a few minutes, the main hatch opened and a head popped out to see how we were. One of the fellows who was asleep on the couch fell to the handrail in the ceiling, breaking it, but not his arm.

Clair was able to resew the damage on the head of the main sail. When she was done, it was like new. She then went to her cabin and we did not see her for a day. Bob gave the order that we could no longer leave coffee grounds laying around, because we were picking them up for the rest of the cruise.

This strangely was not the scariest part of the trip, because the whole incident was probably five minutes. The worst part of the trip was the tropical thunderstorm—we could see the clouds for a couple of days. At first, they were just on the horizon, but each day they were higher. With a 62-foot mast, it is not the most comforting feeling to go through a three-hour thunderstorm. It was flash-boom every five to ten seconds. I'm told a properly grounded boat should survive this type of storm. However, I have heard of holes being blown out of the bottoms of boats, but maybe they weren't properly grounded. I just recently heard of a toilet being blown apart, because of an accumulation of sewer gas.

The last strange thing about this trip was the clothes that I was wearing during the knock down would not dry out, even leaving them out in the tropical sun for a couple of days. Clair told me I would not get them dry until I soaked them in fresh water to get the salt out of them. I did not want to waste the fresh water, so I waited till we got into port with an unlimited amount of fresh water—problem solved.

When we get back and are flying home, we get to the airport and at the check-in desk, we are told we have too much luggage. We were two pieces over our limit and we have to pay extra for those extra pieces. Bob pointed out that a couple of pieces were very small. The nice gentleman was just doing his job, so he said, "I'm sorry, but it's not the size that matters—only the number of pieces. Bob gets out his duct tape and proceeds to tape two small pieces to two other small pieces and we are legal.

Years later, I pull out a t-shirt Clair had made up in memory of our trip. The name of the boat was Cheers:

Cheers, Annapolis, to St. Thomas October 18-28, 1992, 12.22 knots (our average speed), Herb southbound, 18d degrees 3 minutes north 64 degrees, 50 minutes west. New friends, great memories (!?!) MQ Break*** More to follow, November Mike November. Wallow, Wallow, Wallow. D.H. The three-dog day. P.F. When you see the Southern Cross for the first time C. S. & N. Have a good watch, Herb South Bound!! I've changed the flight to Friday. B.R. luggage Anyone? "Her Oinkness" B.C.

I am not going to try to explain everything on the t-shirt. However, I will say it was one of the most memorable trips of my Life's Journey. When I wear it, it means nothing to anybody else, except for the six people who own one.

I have lost touch with most of the them and Bob has passed on to the great sailboat going over the horizon looking for the green flash! Three of us had our Captain's license, Clair was the daughter of a sailmaker, and Clair and the other two guys were avid sailboat racers.

Captain's licenses are complicated; There is the license for the launch at the yacht club and there is the six pack that limits you to six passengers, the 100 ton that requires knowledge of celestial navigation and goes up to a vessel of 100 tons. Then it goes up to cruise ships and tankers and freighters—even the people that work in the engine rooms require a special license. So when you are taking the test, it is generally all day. Only one part of it is limited to one hour—the rest has no time limit and some of it allows you to use reference books and are labeled a to z, because there are 26 of them. While I was taking the one-hour test, a fellow in front of me asks a question of the proctor about fifty minutes into that part of the test and he was still on Question 1. The proctor said he could not help him on that particular question and then said he only had ten minutes for the other nine questions. The fellow then slams his book shut, gets up, and walks out.

I got a lot of my charters from referrals, but most of my charters were from Sail Boston. My charters were mostly local and they were usually for engagements, dispersal of cremated ashes, sightseeing, and occasional short trips down to Cape Cod or Martha's Vineyard. This was not a profession, because I could not start to pay my expenses. As I have said before, I still worked for Sears and could work a pretty flexible schedule with thirty years seniority. I did enjoy the people I met, because they just wanted to go out and have a nice day on the water.

One interesting trip was booked by the employees of the Tap in Boston. They had booked an afternoon out to the Outer Islands and then as an anniversary present for their bosses, they booked a trip down to Martha's Vineyard to visit a fellow who had inherited a fair amount of money—he had been the Taps bouncer. He had bought a bed and breakfast with his inheritance and the group wanted them to go down to visit him. When we got there, he related a story of having received a call from Carly Simon to put up some of her friends, because she was doing some remodeling. While they were working out the arrangements, his two-year-old son decided to throw a terrible two's tantrum. She asked if he was his son and he said yes and apologized for his actions. Carly picked him up in her lap and started to sing to him. It seems the son recognized greatness and he just sat there and stared at her in awe, never realizing he was getting his own personal concert.

On our way back to Boston, the weather got nasty and I could tell my charter's girlfriend was not feeling well. I asked her if she would like to get off at the closest port, which was Plymouth, Massachusetts. She said yes, so they call her sister on their cell phone. The sister agrees to come pick her up. I thought my charter would get off with her, but he said he would go back with me. As we get back out in Massachusetts Bay, I notice he is looking behind me with a strange look on his face. I looked back and about eight feet off my starboard side, swimming beside us is a great white shark that appeared to be fifteen to sixteen feet long.

I have since read it's not like *Jaws* and it wants to attack you—they are just curious. It is the only one I have ever seen and it was impressive. I felt honored to have had this experience. I think I might have witnessed the beginning of the great whites coming north because of the increase of seals in New England. Also, I have a comment on the number of shark attacks all over the country—most recently in Maine. In New England, the Gulf Stream will occasionally eddy in close to New England and bring warmer waters. But around the country, they are finding where fishermen are, there is bait. The sharks are actually coming closer to shore, because of more oxygen in the water than off-shore. After that, the rest of the trip was anticlimactic.

I have had whales, basking sharks, dolphins, and killer whales surface next to me, but nothing more improvised than a great white shark.

One of the strangest things was during a night passage off Georgia, I get this thump on my chest and I realize I had just been hit by a flying fish that is flapping around in my lap. Being soft-hearted, I pick him up and throw him back. In my kindness, I had a smell on my hands that I could not get out for two days.

When a night passage is made during a full moon, it is eerily moving and almost like daytime—especially when the rest of the crew is asleep. Also, any time at night with the phosphorus churning out behind the boat, it makes it look like it is powered by a silent rocket.

Another experience at night that I am told is if you smell like you are next to a garbage truck, it is really a whale with bad breath. I have not had this pleasure or lack of it. I have only been told about it from my boating buddies.

The tall ships have been in Boston Harbor several times, but one time there was about 130 of them. The viewing boats are going in a procession up and down each set of piers and it is very crowded. As I'm coming up on one, I did not notice that one of the vessels had not set his yardarms at an angle and the vessel behind me hailed me to look up. My mast was heading straight for his yardarm. I was able to pull out just in time. All the other ships had offset their yardarms at an angle, but I do not know why this one had not.

When I return to the marina and dock the boat, I get a standing ovation from the upstairs bar.

I had been doing this for twenty years and this had never happened before. I go up to one of my friends and asked what was the standing "O" for. He told me that a boat had just come in before me and hit three boats and bounced off a dock trying to dock. I found out he was a transient who did not know about the currents in the marina, when the Charles River locks were open.

A fellow contacts me to bring him out to one of the islands for his engagement on the boat at anchor. I tell him he should have the boat for the night and that I will go ashore and camp on Rainsford Island. He says he has a tent that I can use, so we're good. He comes looking for me on the night that we had arranged. He found one of my friends who knew what was going on. My friend looks down and comments on his patent leather shoes, because it was a special occasion. I go ashore and pitch the tent, but I did not know a gale was coming, so I slept on the island. The next morning, when I get up, everything must have gone well, because I look down and they are swimming off the stern of the boat. It seems they could not figure out the shower, but she was very happy.

I do not know how many people work in Boston, but a couple of months later, I got another charter. The people tell me they knew and worked with the couple that got engaged out at Rainsford. I do not know if they came looking for me to go on the same boat their friends had chartered or if it was just a strange coincidence. I do know it wasn't to get engaged.

A guy at the marina bar wants to bring his girlfriend out for an evening sail and, for whatever reason, he wants me to act like we are old friends. As we meet, he says he forgot something and has to go back to his car and leaves his girlfriend with me. She was standing there and says, "You don't know him from Adam." I just smiled. As we are sailing out into the night from the harbor, he asks if there is any way to have some privacy. I said you can go below and put the washboards in. Bata Bing; Bata Bang, and they are gone. Three hours later, his head pops out of the cabin asking where are we. I guess this was better than getting a room.

One of my most favorite charters were six college kids from MIT. They were from all over the world, so each one spoke a different language. They were given a choice of going to Newport, Rhode Island, to tour the mansions or go sailing. I guess they were all used to mansions. Since they were all fantastic sailors, they chose to go sailing in Boston Harbor. I let each one sail the boat and between the six of them, somebody was able to interpret for somebody else to ask a question or say what they wanted to say. They were the most fantastic kids! If they are our future, we are in good hands.

CHAPTER 14

Power Squadron and Maine Sailing

When I got involved in teaching with the Power Squadron, one of the courses was cruise planning. The last chapter was how to protect yourself away from the coast. Many people are not aware of the number of pirates out there that will come across a lone sailor and kill him for his vessel. These thugs that are out there running drugs do not go into a boat show and buy a boat. Knowing how to protect yourself is critical. Drug dealers are not necessarily looking for go-fast boats either—with the cabin gutted to hold more drugs, a sailboat will work just as well and is less conspicuous.

Knowing how to protect yourself is critical. The best way to make a passage is with a group of boats. With safety in numbers, the other is carrying the weapons needed, like the old rumrunner, I met as a child in Portsmouth, Rhode Island. The important thing to remember is carry a cannon, aka the largest rifle you can, so they cannot stand just outside your range and keep on firing at you. If you show them you have the firepower, they will generally leave you alone.

Another weapon you should have is a stainless-steel pistol or revolver. As we are covering this last part of the chapter, one friend reminds me that I recommend to always carry a weapon at sea and on land. Another friend challenges this statement, and asks emphatically, "Always?"

The first guy states firmly, "Yes, always," and then reaches into the back of his waist and pulls out a very impressive stainless-steel pistol.

The challenger says, "No shit, that's the same as mine," and pulls out a duplicate from his boot. These guys were quite law-abiding people and I had known both of them for over ten years, but never knew either one of them was packing heat. One was even a school bus driver and won an award for being foster father of the year.

One day, I was sailing with two other boats in Maine in the fog. The last boat comes over the radio and says the dingy that he had been towing had slipped it's painter. He was going back to look for it, because it had not been long since he had last noticed it was still there and it was new. We all said we would turn around and help him in a sweep side-by-side to look for it.

Meanwhile the fog closes in even more so, and as we are doing the sweep, we lose track of each other. After about an hour, our buddy calls back and says never mind, so we then try to relocate each other with our latitude and longitude readings from GPS readings. Meanwhile, a couple of down Mainers are enjoying the entertainment coming over their radios. One says to the other, "First he loses his dingy— then he loses his buddies." That kind of wrapped it all up with some down Maine humor. Down Mainers are about as dry as you can get them and still be on the water. One day I hear one calling his buddy in the fog, "You out?" About five minutes later, a reply came—"Yup."

Sailing in the fog can be hazardous, so you must have radar to help with the hazards. The first time I went to Maine, all I had was LORAN C, which I thought was pretty good getting from point A to B. It had its flaws though. One was you could not see what might be in your way and two, it used signals from three land stations that were subject to electronic interference. This system was deemed obsolete February 8, 2010.

When we were up by Jonesboro, Maine, and knew we wanted to go to the left, we started bearing to port. After about six miles, with the fog burning off or as the down Mainers say, "Scaling up," we realize we were way off course. The interference was extreme from submarine station broadcasting towers close by in Cutler, Maine. They operate at a very low frequency with a signal of NAA at 24 KHZ from towers that are 800 to a 1,000 feet tall and cover all of the Atlantic. When I got back, the first order of business was to get a radar unit. Problem solved!

While sailing in Booth Bay Harbor, we were having a lovely time with another sailboat right beside us. Anybody that has sailed knows whether you know the people in the boat next to you or not, it is a friendly race. As we are enjoying this little nautical challenge, a cigarette boat, aka loud, fast, gas guzzler, goes flying past us and the other fellow yells over, "Now we have something to aspire to." For some reason, whenever I see a power boat, I'll always remember that comment.

Before I had a sailboat, one of the fellows I worked with had one that he kept in Portsmouth Harbor in New Hampshire. He invited me to go sailing with him one day. As we sailed through the harbor, we passed the Portsmouth Naval Prison that held Navy's misfits from all over the world. They were just sitting there by their windows watching us. It seemed a very strange line between freedom and incarnation. Time has passed and this prison that is actually in Kittery, Maine, is still in limbo after closing in 1974 after having held 86,000 men.

CHAPTER 15

Creatures Domestic and Wild

Storing my Catalina 30 sailboat was easy. I had two guys that owned a trucking company called Marine Traders haul me back and forth every spring and fall from Marblehead to Tewksbury.

When in Tewksbury, it sat next to my garage. There I could work on it at my leisure, whether I had an extra hour or a day. The shipping cost was less than winter storage wherever I stored it. I did not have to drive fifty miles each way whenever I wanted to work on it. If I wanted to just sit and have a beer and relax, it was there.

The bow sat about ten feet above the ground, because of the high keel and jack stands. It was right next to an arborvitae bush that was about thirteen feet high. A robin would come in and land on the bow and hop over to her nest. She had many baby robins throughout the years. You are probably wondering why I knew it was the same robin. This bird had a white birth mark on her head that looked like another bird had pooped on her. I called her Gorbachev.

I had other birds that came back every year. My favorites were the Canadian geese. They nested on a small island that was on the pond in my backyard. The island was perfect because foxes, coyotes, and other varmints could not get to them.

Again, how did I know it was the same geese? At first, it was just a feeling, the way they would approach me every spring, bringing their

goslings up to me like proud parents. Then I did not know it was not legal to feed them. If I did not go down to the pond, they would come up to the house to get me. When I stopped feeding them, they would still come up to me, even the next year. It appears the game warden captured all of them and put large white collars on their necks with numbers you could read with binoculars, along with small bands on their legs. I read about this type of banding in *National Geographic*. I was down by the pond with my 130-pound black lab/golden retriever mix, MacDuff, and my 20-pound yellow tiger cat, Deuce, both of whom loved the water, when the geese decided to join us. You might not find this credible, but somewhere I have two fishermen who were watching us that are telling this same story.

A Maine lobsterman had a seagull (his name was Red Eye) that went out with him every day. One day he notices that something had happened to the bird's foot and he cannot walk on it. This is a death sentence for a seagull! He manages to catch it and bring it to a veterinarian. They were able to fix the foot and gave the bird back to the lobsterman. Now the bird is back with his lobstering buddy.

My wife comes home from the supermarket and says she could not figure out what the birds were doing in the parking lot as she watched them. It was a hot dry day and they were under the cars with their heads lifted up under the engines. She finally figured out that they drinking the condensation from the cars' air conditioners.

The last story of a bird that came back every year was a little hummingbird. I recognized him by the fact that all summer long, he would be at the feeder. In the fall, I noticed he had not been around for a couple of weeks. I tell the wife and she brings the feeder in, cleans it up, and stores it for the next year. Next year, I look out and the little guy is hovering where the feeder was last year. Welcome home!

Yes, I miss my northern friends as I sit here in my retirement home in southwest Florida. My chair is next to a full window with a cardinal looking in at me about three feet away. I have to accept I can't be in both places at the same time. My southern friends are a hawk, about twenty pounds, a three-foot-tall crane, and at least four marsh bunnies—may be more—I can never get a good count, because they are all over the place.

Also, I have two four-foot long black racer snakes, and about six osprey nests on the street, with a bald eagle nest about one half mile from here. What I do have here that I had up north are squirrels eating weeds and acting like it is catnip—I guess it's squirrel nip .My doggies and cat have gone to pet heaven, but I have inherited a feral cat I feed, but cannot get within eight feet of him. Also, because I have to feed the cat outside, we have a vulture that likes to eat cat food, who lurks nearby. I think I have found a place where I can feed the cat that the vulture does not like. I keep remembering other critters that come and go—a snapping turtle, woodpeckers, doves, and a lot of little geckos that all have favorite spots. Fortunately, I have not had to deal with my neighbor's alligator or python.

I started this section of my story with storing my sailboat at home, but after I sold it, I bought a 34-foot Mariner Trawler. This could not be trucked over the road, unless I took off the flybridge, which was expensive, so the fellows that hauled my sailboat rented an empty lot on the Merrimac River in Newburyport, where I could store it without shipping it over the road. The first year worked out well, but the next year they said the people that owned the lot doubled their price. Apparently after seeing they had filled the lot, which was about three acres, they got greedy.

I went back to the marina that I had first done business with about thirty years ago on Rings Island with the Halcyon directly across from Newburyport still on the Merrimac River. They say I can store it there, so it will just be pulled out and set beside the ramp. A couple of years later, I drive by the lot I was in, but it is still empty. Isn't it strange how greed can empty a pocket? With the boat on the Merrimac across from Newburyport, it was like having waterfront property in the spring while I worked on it. In the summer, I went back to Shipyard Quarters in Charlestown.

CHAPTER 16

Boston

M uch of what I have written already is about Boston and boating there. However, many other things about this city are fascinating, but I cannot possibly cover everything—Boston is a book in itself, if not volumes. I will cover a little of my journey around and about it. The only tall building I remember when I came back from out west was the Custom House Tower. It has a great bar on the second floor. I believe it's still open to the public, because the Custom House is now owned by Marriot as condos. The city is really a great walking city, marked by a red brick path called the Freedom Trail. It has a beautiful park like New York City called the Common.

It was originally a cow pasture and a staging area for revolutionary troops. At the end of the Common is the capitol with its gold dome. I found it fascinating that my father had a friend who took him up in the dome. I don't think this could be done today.

After I got married, there was a restaurant in our back bay called 9 Knox Street. I googled it and, as I expected, it's no longer in business, but it is legendary to the history of Boston eateries. It was run by Jeffery W. Davis and I believed he had a partner who helped him. It was a small elegant restaurant with the same name as its address and only operated during the seventies.

Reservations took three to six months and the menu was basically a softball-sized slice of Beef Wellington. Dessert was 9 Knox pie, a graham-cracker-crusted affair filled with fresh fruit, whipped cream, and chocolate. The table was also memorable—a solid cross cut off a very old tree fifty-four inches round. The story went that a tree of this size was supposed to go back to England before the revolution for the masts for ships, so this table was historic contraband. Like the recreation of the last meal on the Titanic, this was one of my most memorable dining experiences.

Like every memorable city, Boston has many great restaurants. Another of my favorites was the Top of the Hub, aka the Prudential Tower. Here you can be seated and overlook all of the city and the harbor and watch the planes take off from Logan Airport at eye-level or look out twenty to thirty miles to the horizon.

Boston's dining is so varied that I had a couple of friends that went out every Friday night, and never went back to the same restaurant in a span of twenty years. However, they would go back if a restaurant had closed and reopened under a new name. For those who like an adult beverage, this can also be the case. My friends would go back to their favorites on a different night. My brother-in-law lived in northern Ohio and he was so excited when a new restaurant just opened, so we went with him—it was a disaster. When he came up to Boston, it blew his mind.

Charlestown is an interesting part of Boston, which is about one square mile, where the Charles River flows into the harbor through a set of locks. However, this is not where the show, *Cheers*, takes place. It's right across from the Common, aka the Bull and Finch Pub, but it's another spot where everyone knows your name. A couple of my favorite spots were Harbor Watch, which has the best view of the city and has been remodeled several times with several changes of name, and the Warren Tavern—I do not think it has changed in its two hundred and thirty years. It's one of the oldest taverns in our country.

One of the first times I was at the Marina Bar, there were two guys sitting next to me talking about their experiences in jail, like it was normal. This is where the movie, *The Town*, was filmed. If you have not seen it, you might like it. I found it a very realistic portrayal of Charlestown. I do not want to say everyone in Charlestown is a bank robber, but it is one of the main professions.

The Marina Bar was like a lot of local bars around the country, where you could just start talking to the person next to you. Here I have to change a name—I'll call him "Sam," but my source is very reliable. A prominent businessman likes to come in for an adult beverage by himself. This girl starts talking to him about Sam and the conversation turns to her knowing that Sam lives in the condo next to the marina. She says that he occasionally lands his helicopter on Pier 5. Then she starts talking about all the businesses he owns. After going on about fifteen minutes, she takes a breath and introduces herself. Then she asks him for his name. His reply—Sam.

I'm sitting on my boat, when I hear a firetruck coming down the street that the marina is on, but I cannot see anything wrong. The problem is on the next street over, so instead of going around the rotary and driving over to the next street, they take off over the walk that is above the water. It seems that the walk was designed just for people—not fire trucks, even though it was a short cut. Fortunately, they were going fast enough not to fall through, but it broke every board in the pier.

I did enjoy the Marina Bar and one of my buddies even lived on a boat there. The marina only had one black man (Black John), but I believe his last name was Mc Elroy, though I think I'm spelling it wrong. John was a vet, who must have had a very important job in the service, because I overheard him talking to another fellow about it and it was way over my head.

John and I were sitting at the bar and like my other friend, John would say, "We were swapping stories and telling lies." Along comes another fellow from the marina and he sits down beside me. He buys me a drink, but doesn't buy one for John.

John looks at him and simply asks, "What am I—black?"

Another night John and I are relaxing at the bar and it is unusually quiet. John asks me if I like jazz and the blues. I reply, "Does a bear do poopy in the woods?" Before you can sing the first line of *Take the A Train* by Duke Ellington, we are on our way to one of the best jazz clubs in Boston—if not the country, Wally's. John was very well-known there and he introduced me to all his friends—his lawyer, dentist, the owner (who was Wally's son) and the leader of the band.

I know I'm forgetting a couple of people. The owner asked where I was parked and I said out front. He said it would be safer around back, so we went out and he unlocked the back lot and put me in his parking space. Every time John would introduce me to one of his friends, they would ask how he got there and he would say Paul brought me. Then that person would buy me a drink and another shot glass would be put upside down in front of me. That meant I had one coming. It was an interesting night and place. You have probably figured it out. I was the only pearly white face there. It was one of the best times I have ever had in a Boston night club and the owner got us a cab at closing.

The next morning, I wake up thinking about what had happened there. That's when all the pieces started to fit together. John's jeep had been setting on the pier for quite a while, so everyone was asking how he had landed there and wondered how he was doing. I knew Wally had died not long ago. Apparently, John had gotten drunk at Wally's wake and lost his license.

John was one of the few people I ever knew who suffered from shell shock, aka, "combat fatigue" or "nervous in the service." Being relatively close, every night when the Constitution fired its cannon at sunset, John would hit the floor, even knowing it was coming. He could not control this reaction. John is gone now. I really miss him, as I tell these stories with a tear in my eye.

One of my favorite islands is out by Boston Light. Calf Island is uninhabited now, but in the past, people did live on it. It is just a rookery for seagulls now and they do get upset when you impose on their island. I didn't go out there often, because of upsetting the birds—they know how to buzz you from behind.

One day I brought a neighbor out and we are walking along a very small beach. Suddenly, I spot a bottle sporting a pink ribbon with black polka dots tied around its neck, screaming to be picked up. It is the only bottle with a note in it that I have ever found—it had been dropped in the water in Naples, Florida. That is only about thirty miles from where I now live. I think this was done in March and I found the bottle in the summer. It was carried by the Gulf Stream and had a girl's name and address written on the note. My wife is a teacher, so she wrote back to her with an assignment that she should look up Calf Island to see the history of the island where her bottle was found.

The girl did write back and thanked us for replying. She told us that her note had gone the farthest of anyone else's note.

Several times while I kept my boat in Charlestown, a repair ship named the USS Sierra AD 18 came into Boston. The marina that I was docked in was the old Charlestown Navy Yard. The first time the Sierra came into Charlestown, I recognized it as one of the ships my father had been stationed on. I called him up and asked if he would like to come in and see it. He hesitated and then said no, because he did not want to deal with Boston's traffic. I said OK and left it at that.

Then I thought about it the next year when it was back again. I called him up again and when he gives me the traffic excuse, I said I would come out and get him, so he wouldn't have to worry about the traffic. By the time I picked him up and got back, it was late in the day. We walk over and go up the gang plank, because it had been open to the public. The officer of the day says, "I am sorry, but visiting hours are over."

My father simply says, "That's OK, I know what it looks like," and turns around to walk down the ramp. When we get back on the dock, he walks to the stern of the ship and says, "It's still there." I was puzzled by what he meant. He said that while they were tied to the dock in China, the dock had caught fire. Before they could get the ship untied and under way, the heat from the dock had warped the steel plates. He was amazed they had never replaced them. This happened from October 1945 through February 1946, which was when the ship was stationed in Shanghai.

Being a machinist on this ship, he used to make silencers for the men on watch to shoot rats on the pier. The other ship story he told me was that while they were tied up to the pier, it was not uncommon to see bodies floating down the river. I just saw a special on COVID-19 on CNN—China has really changed. The Sierra was commissioned out of Tampa, Florida, in February 1945 and decommissioned in October 1993. That means it was the second oldest warship of the United States in our country, the oldest, a stone's throw away, being The USS Constitution, aka Old Ironsides.

CHAPTER 17

Neighbors

Everybody has neighbor stories and mine are probably not any stranger than yours. I have lived all over the country and when I was a child, neighbors never meant much to me. Friends in high school meant a lot more to me, but I do not remember even one of my neighbors while I was in high school.

Now I am living in Florida with great neighbors, but I look back at my neighborhood where I lived for forty years and many were strange and just as many were fantastic. I'm going to tell stories of the strange ones, because nice neighbor stories are boring. Although I will touch on some of my nice neighbors, most of these tales will be of the strange ones.

Buying the house in Tewksbury started off weirdly. We were visiting the people that had lived upstairs from us when we got married. We had to use their bathroom when we returned from our honeymoon, because our bathroom was full of newspaper. My wife had worked with her. Then they moved to the next town and we later moved there, too, only a couple of streets over. Then they moved to Tewksbury and when we went to visit them, Tony said the house across the street that was being built was for sale and the builder lived two doors over. I go over and talk to Johnny, the builder, and he says he has sold the house, but if anything comes up, he will let Tony know.

A couple of days later, Tony calls me and says Johnny wants to see me. When I go over, Johnny says, "Paul, if you want this house, it's yours."

I said, "I'll take it" and asked what happened to the first deal. It seems that Johnny tells the realtor who happens to live between the two houses (the one I am trying to buy and Johnny's) that he has sold the house and the realtor asks to whom. Johnny tells him and the agent says that he already showed the house to those people. so now Johnny has to pay the agent the commission. Before Johnny does that, he asks the people if the agent had showed them the house, but they said he did not. Johnny says somebody is lying and I don't have to figure out who.

After we move into the house, the realtor has his son throwing rocks at the side of our house. Then his wife dies and the bank forecloses on his house, because of gambling debts—all within a couple of months. We learn this from the people who bought his house—their banker told them about his gambling problems.

Now the neighbor on the other side is shooting a pistol off his back porch and I don't know if he is shooting at my cat or what in the dark. When he goes on business trips, his wife is making stag films with the local highway department, as witnessed by my other neighbor's peeping Tom son. One day the kids are going to school and in walking past this house, they see that a drunken half-naked body is lying in the front yard. My friend, Tony, asks me if I want to change their front porch light to red. I told him that was not a good idea. Fortunately, that neighbor only lasted about half a year.

The new neighbor was all right, except when he had cookouts. Then he would light firecrackers and throw them to his dog to catch in his mouth. Tony's son said he was over to the new neighbor's house when he had built a bonfire up against a four-foot boulder, Tony's son asked him what he was doing and he said he was trying to burn it, so he could put in a pool.

Meanwhile Johnny, the builder, has built a fish cage in the pond in his backyard, but after a heavy rain, the water goes over the top and all his fish swim away. Then he gets two sheep and shortly after, he slaughters one. The other one just runs around bleating until Johnny could not stand it, so he slaughters the second one.

Across from Johnny diagonally from me lived Jimmie and Sue and to their left Chuck and Judy—all great people. Chuck is the only one still left and I think I have said Chuck lives about one hundred thirty miles from where I am now. I have kept in touch with him. He even went on my intercoastal trip that I will talk about later. Chuck and I still get together and we always end up telling Jimmie stories, because he was truly old school Italian.

Down the street lived a kid who was just trouble. Once he came into my yard because his dog was chasing my cat. I told him to get himself and his dog out of my yard. He yelled back at me, "I will go wherever I want and I don't care if my dog kills your cat!"

I had a shovel leaning against the house, which I picked it up, so I could finish him (about the only time I have ever been this mad). I relate my story to Jimmie and he says he has had a problem with this same thug, always speeding up the street. And the old school Italian comes out, as he says, "Let's whack him." Sometime later, I am talking to a Tewksbury cop about this thug and ask whatever happened to him. The cop says that he is doing time in the big house. YES! What goes around comes around!

I liked Jimmie, so one night his wife, Sue, calls me and says come quick—Jimmie is going to kill somebody!! She also tells me to bring the dog (my one-hundred-thirty-pound beast). A kid had just walked into his house and Jimmie, protecting his daughter, pinned the kid against a wall. Sue does not think to call the police, but because I'm closer, she calls me, because I'll get there before he kills the kid. The kid was drunk and came from the party down the street. After we got all that resolved, the kid never came back.

As the years go by, Johnny (the contractor) leaves his wife, which I think is a great idea. Then she takes in boarders, which is not legal within our zoning. These boarders had taken a taxi home, but said they lived in my house and they had to go into my house to get the money to pay the taxi driver his fare. Now I come home and there is a taxi setting in my driveway and the taxi cab driver had to have been waiting quite a while for his fare.

I told him I would go in and check with my wife. She said she had heard something, but nobody had come to the door. I told the taxi cab driver there was no one there and I was not paying his fare. If he wanted, either he or I could call the police. He finally gave up and left. We finally figured it out—it was the wacky witch's boarders.

The couple that bought the real estate agent's house were great neighbors. They raised miniature schnauzers and at times had eight to sixteen dogs and puppies. It seems that Johnny's wife found out that the code for Tewksbury was no more than three dogs for less than four acres. Yet her with two illegal tenants, she had the nerve to file a complaint against him with the town. He, being the nice guy he was, never brought up her illegal tenants or her defecating in the backyard.

When we get back from our road trip, which I will cover in the next chapter, Lennie calls us up and asks us if we would like one of the dogs. He was down to eight and we had been without one for about a year, so he thought we might be interested in having one. We go over and ask which one he would part with. He said, "These two are the oldest, so they would be the hardest to find homes for.

I said, "We'll take them—they're small and will keep each other company." I then asked him how he would handle the other six. He said he would only put three outside at a time. Johnny's wife would not be able to tell the difference.

Both of our dogs were female. One was named Champion Foxy Lady and the other was called Champion Cotton Candy. We decided not to change their names, but just call them Foxy and Candy. A funny side note was Foxy's father was a champion, but his registered name was ugly from the front. They just called him Lyle for Lyle Lovett—sorry, Lyle.

I always have had large dogs, but when they got older, I had to carry them up the stairs to the bedroom and back down in the morning. They would not sleep downstairs by themselves. In our old age, the smaller dogs worked out much better, especially as we started our snowbirding, aka driving north and south over the years—they really traveled well. Now I can say I have two lap girls, Foxy and Candy. The only problem with having two miniature schnauzers is that it's tough having two dogs that are smarter than you. They could work me to a frazzle.

However, having a big dog can be an advantage. One day my boss asked if I could go into the warehouse and pick up a load of air conditioners, because of a delivery strike and we were in the middle of a heat wave. I said sure and got the truck and went home and picked up my 130-pound beast, aka MacDuff. When I got to the warehouse, I rolled the windows down halfway and let MacDuff protect me.

I pull up to the dock and the warehouse guy asked how did I run the strike line. As MacDuff is going bonkers trying to get to him, he looks at the dog and says, "Oh, I see." While he was having the air conditioners loaded, he asked if I would like a tour of the warehouse. Knowing this might be the only time this could happen (salespeople were not supposed to be in the warehouse), I said yes.

The bays were four high with an opening of about seven feet. He clamped me into a safety harness and off we go. Each time we went to another level, the forklift would go slower at the fourth level. It would not move and he tells me, "Do not step back, as we are at about twenty-eight feet up. One sad thing about this strike was it really closed this warehouse—it is now a shopping mall in Dorchester, Massachusetts.

When I was younger, I really enjoyed the pond I lived on and in the winter, we would skate on its seventy acres. I love to hear the ice crack on cold nights as it expanded. Crazy Gary of Whitewater Rafting and Rye fishing fame would come over. We would go down to the other end of the pond, hold a sheet between us, and fly back down. The one scary part was not letting your skates get caught in the cracks in the ice.

I used to have Super Bowl parties. We skated until the game started and then went in to watch it. One year, one of the guys fell on the ice. I cannot remember if he broke something, but I do remember the ambulance was called. We had brought him through the bulkhead into the bar. When the EMTs showed up, they looked around and asked what was going on.

We also had bowling parties and I had a tap system. We started off with a quarter keg of beer and kept on getting more beer, because we always ran out. Towards the end, we were up to two half kegs, aka a full barrel of beer (sixty-four gallons).

On one of our bowling parties, we were down by the pond. Somebody yelled that two guys had just tipped over and they didn't have life preservers on. I had two canoes and the other was right there. I asked for somebody to go out with me and one of the women grabbed a paddle and we were off. I still remember my chauvinist thought of needing a guy to go out with me.

The second we started, I realized my canoe partner was better than anybody I had ever been partnered with in a canoe. We got out super-fast, righted the canoe beside us, and held the gunnels next to ours, so they could climb back into their canoe. When we get back in, I had to ask Betty how she had become such a great canoeist. She said she had been a camp counselor and canoe instructor for years.

The rest of the story: one of the fellows we saved ended up becoming her husband the next year. How great is that? Strangely, when my mother passed away, Betty worked for the town in which my mother passed away, so she handled the death certificate.

CHAPTER 18

Road Trip

Before we get the schnauzers. Foxy and Candy, I retire. My wife had already retired, so I told her I had always wanted to take a road trip around the country.

I had seen a lot of the country with my Power Squadron conventions, but having lived on the West Coast as a child, there was a lot I had not seen or could not remember. We did not know where we were going or how long we would be gone, so we asked our lifelong friends and neighbors across the street, Tony and Carol, if they would mind getting our mail and paying any bills we had coming that were not auto-pay. I gave them a book of blank checks, all pre-signed. How many people have friends and neighbors you can do that with? They were closer than family.

A side note here is that we had no children, but they had a son and daughter, so we got to experience children without the expense of college and bringing them up. When they were older and we were going out with Tony and Carol, we would leave my 130-pound strike runner (MacDuff) with the kids for protection and we were off.

Our first stop was my wife's brother, Bill, in Arnold, Maryland, just outside Annapolis. Our next stop was another brother outside of Lexington, Virginia. Then we went down the coast to a cousin in Jacksonville, Florida and after that, Chuck, an old neighbor that I have already talked about. All of this we had done many times, so it was old hat.

Then we started with the new stuff. Our first stop after Chuck's was Cedar Key, Florida. We should go back to see it again someday, because when we were there, the fog was so thick, I thought I was back in Maine. We were walking along the dock, when we noticed a couple heading into a little restaurant. They looked at us and said, "Dog night." This sounded interesting, so we followed them in and found hot dogs were a dollar apiece and beer was $2.50, with no charge for a salad or dessert, since they had been provided by the waitresses. The whole night came to $16, including the 20% tip.

From here we head for Mobile, Alabama, and one of the most impressive Christmas displays I have ever seen. I think it was on the estate of a Coca Cola executive.

Then we were off to Branson, Missouri. I had always heard about Branson and did not know what to expect. The entertainment met my expectation, but I was not ready for the gorgeous hills and valleys. I thought it was a strange place for entertainment, but when you think about it, it is centrally located. Who would have thought a place like Las Vegas sitting in the middle of a desert would draw people like it does.

Now we are off to my wife's sister's place in Norman, Oklahoma. This is another place I thought would be flat land, but it had nice rolling hills. She had always questioned why we moved to a place that had so many hurricanes, yet she lives in Tornado Alley! While she had her house being built, she went and checked the storm shelter. When she saw the door opened outward, she asked the builder, "What if the door is blocked by debris?"

He said, "I never thought of that." I think he now builds shelters with the door opening inward.

As we traveled around the country, I always went to local ATMs for cash. While we were here, I went to a little local variety store about three miles from her house. Later that spring, we saw displayed on the national news a picture of that same variety store, but it was just rubble from a tornado. The people who worked there had gone into the meat locker that had been built for the store's shelter.

A strange thing about Norman was they hardly ever got snow. Most people there did not even own a snow shovel. While we were visiting, they were pounded with about ten inches of snow. I carried a snow shovel with me, remembering what had happened to George C. Scott, so I helped shovel them out.

From there we headed south to San Antonio, Texas. This is an absolutely lovely city with an impressive Riverwalk and Tower of America. We were there on New Year's Eve and decided to eat outside. It grew really cold, so we ate our dinners while wrapped in massive Indian blankets, supplied by the restaurant. (they had done this before). Yes, the meal got cold as we dined, but we were warm. The next day, we visited the Alamo and then headed west to Pecos, Texas, with our GPS telling us to go 350 miles—nothing else and no turns.

After Pecos, we travel to Carlsbad Caverns and like Mammoth Caves. they are spectacular. Leaving the caves, we took a little side trip and having a Prius with a very quiet engine, we ended up right next to a little red fox that did not even know we were four feet away from him. The little guy was just sitting there by us.

On this note, I have a Rav4 and the wife's car is a Prius. I had to learn to toot my horn when coming up on people walking the other way from me on the same side of the street, because they do not know I am there. I have heard Toyota is thinking about giving the car some sort of special sound people can hear to let them know something is coming up behind them.

We are now off to Roswell, New Mexico, and Area 51. This is another place in the middle of nowhere and like Loch Ness in Scotland, the people there know how to draw the tourists. They do have some pretty convincing evidence, but what I got the biggest kick out of was their spaceman street lights with Santa hats. I also enjoy the TV show, *The Secret of Skinwalker Ranch*, and after my great blackout stories of November 9, 1965, I think you know how I feel about this area.

The next stop is Tombstone, Arizona. Why anybody would want to be there and have a gun fight is beyond me. It took me forever to get there by car, let alone what it would have taken to get there by horse. Getting out of Tombstone as soon as possible, we are off to visit friends In Sedona, Arizona. These are people I met through one of my cousins. Twenty-five years ago, I had been to Sedona with my brother-in-law, when we were hiking the Grand Canyon.

The last time I was there, it was a little wilder and like now, the pink jeep drivers pack revolvers. The story goes (and I am sure there is some truth to it) that the revolvers are to shoot rattlesnakes, but I still think it is mostly show for the tourists. The pink jeep drivers are great tour guides, but to stay with somebody who is a resident is really the way to see Sedona. The word is out—the people of Hollywood love Sedona and it is definitely a place to see some incredible cars.

Now it's off to my favorite ship—the Queen Mary in Long Beach, California. Back about forty years ago, my uncle brought me over to his brother Jean's antique shop in Acton, Massachusetts. I was in awe of what he had. He asked if I saw anything that I liked. I had spotted a five-foot plank on a frame model of the Queen Mary. I have only seen one like it and that one is over the bar at the Sheraton Hotel at Logan airport. I asked the bartender what Sheraton had spent on it and he said he did not know, but he did know that it was big bucks. Jean said he would sell it to me for what he had paid for it. I said, "Sold." It was not big bucks.

The fascination of this grand old vessel is an interesting story. My wife, having been born in Norwich, England, came to this country right after the war, while the Queen was still wearing camouflage and was called the Gray Ghost. The Queen Mary had carried troops during the war, but Hitler's submarines never got her. The ship is now a hotel and function center with an address of 1126 Queens Highway, Long Beach, California and a ZIP Code of 90802. She was retired in 1967. It has an incredible bar up by the bridge and an excellent restaurant in the starboard stern called Sir Winston's. The bathtubs had four faucets. Two hot and cold for fresh water, and two hot and cold for salt water.

While staying there, I thought it would be cool to go down and see Jay Leno, an old neighbor of mine in Hollywood. I lived close to where he lived and I actually think I saw him out jogging once, but I really didn't know him. I feel that he and Johnny Carson were far better late-night hosts than those of today. However, maybe it's just my age—I do not understand the new humor of today.

While staying on the Queen, I remembered an old favorite song of mine, *Santa Catalina*. We took a ferry ride over to the "Island of Romance, twenty-six miles across the sea." It still had a herd of about one hundred and fifty buffalos from old western movies out there. They are considered the farthest west buffalo have ever been in the United States. They are kind of like the feral buffalo of the movie industry. My only regret of staying in this area is that I did not see the Hollywood sign up on the hill. I might have to go back someday.

Now we cut back over to Las Vegas to meet my brother and sister-in-law, who are attending a builder's convention there. We get a call from him and he said he had upgraded our room to one of the top floors of the Flamingo. When we get there, I go into the bathroom and there is a television in the mirror. I look at the mirror—it is only ¼ of an inch thick and the speaker is in the ceiling. I know I have led a sheltered life, but from what I have heard, these are common now. There is not much to say about Las Vegas—they did not build those big hotels with their customers being big winners. I guess you can tell I am not a big gambler, although they do have some great shows.

From here we head for San Simon and the Hearst Castle. If you want to spend the time, there are four full day tours available. We just did the house tour, which is incredible. This is where I learned (being in charge of the supply room) why I had a blank check for our ROTC rifle team. Hearst was a huge supporter of the military and our rifle team was the best high school team in the country—almost all our rifle team graduates went to West Point. To Hearst, he was funding the grass roots.

From the castle, we head north on the coast highway, Route 1. We never realized that the West Coast and the East Coast's coastal highways are both Route 1 from north to south. However, Route 1 on the West Coast joins Route 101 in Leggett, California, and continues as Route 101 to Seattle, Washington.

On our way to San Francisco, I wondered why a lot of the California cities start with San. It is really very simple—the Spanish were there first and they named the cities after saints, which were then shortened to San. We stopped at a fantastic motel at a ragged point about halfway between the castle and the city by the bay. The views along this highway were fantastic, even though we had to deal with some rockslides.

I had been to San Francisco before, but had not been able to get out to Alcatraz. The tour is a little creepy, but very educational and definitely historic, having held some of the most infamous criminals in the country, Al Capone being one. This means while I was in California, I saw two famous rocks—the prison and The Rock, Dwayne Johnson, at the Jay Leno show. Coming back to Massachusetts, we only had one (Plymouth Rock).

We now head for the Avenue of the Giants—appropriately named for the redwoods being the tallest living things in the world. Like the sequoias, they probably took root before Jesus walked this earth. When you are walking next to one that has fallen in a storm, you are walking next to a tree that is longer than a football field. I cannot imagine what it sounded like when it fell or how it felt as the ground shook. These two giants; sequoias and redwoods, have always confused me. Sequoias are fatter and have greater volume, because they are a little wider at the bottom, being able to achieve a diameter of thirty feet. General Sherman is the largest tree in volume and is considered the largest living thing in the world. The redwoods only reach about twenty feet in diameter, but are taller. Having been through both forests, I really can't pick a favorite. The sequoias not only have General Sherman, but you must have see the tree that has been cut out so you can drive a car through it. That is also a sequoia. I think it strange that California has the climate and the soil to grow both of these giants—the sequoias in southern California and the redwoods in the north.

After the giants, we head north and I notice I am getting low on gas. This is something I do not experience with the Prius very often. The strange thing here is there are oil wells pumping all around us. Finally, we come to a little gas station/variety store in Cloverdale, California.

I fill up and pay the cashier, but as I am leaving, I notice a plaque on the wall, "James Dean's Last Stop." I didn't think a lot about this plaque until about thirty miles down the road, where I come to an intersection with another plaque, "James Dean's Memorial Intersection." It was so remote that he did not have a chance. I always thought he was the wild one and was at fault for the accident— wrong! He had the right of way and the other guy ran the stop sign.

Our next stop is Grants Pass, Oregon. This is where our old neighbors had moved. I had not talked about them when I was covering my wacky neighbors, because they were normal, but here is where normal ends. Raj had been the chief go-to guy for a large investment company for their computers and he was going to retire in 1999. The powers that be asked him to stay on till after Y2K, because they did not know what was going to happen with computers. They told him they would make it worth his while to stay on till after the turn of the century.

I do not know what "worth your while" figured out to be,, but I do know he bought a mountaintop that looked down on all of Grants Pass. Their house is over 3,000 square feet and their guest house is 1,000 square feet—when it's not used for guests, it's his wife's quilting and craft house. When he moved there, the local forestry division came to him and asked if they could use his driveway for a command center for fires, because they could look down on everything and it would hold two helicopters. We had a lovely time with our old neighbors, but because of the old saying (guests and fish start to smell after three days), we had to keep moving.

We are off to McMinnville, Oregon, passing through latitude 45 degrees north. This is halfway between the equator and the North Pole. Our destination is Evergreen Aviation and Space Museum. This is a fascinating place that now houses Howard Hughes' Spruce Goose, the largest seaplane ever built. It got its name, because it was all wood—but not spruce. It was made out of plywood and in its hangar, it could house 70 planes underneath it. It was larger than most commercial planes with a wing span of 320 feet and weighing 300,000 pounds. It was designed to carry 700 men. The Spruce Goose is a marvel even today after 70 years. It had eight Pratt and Whitney engines with 28 cylinders that consumed 100 gallons of fuel per hour. It only flew once on November 2, 1947. Its speed would have been 199 mph and its range was about 3,000 miles. The propellers were 17 feet long. In 2001, it cost $25 to get into the cockpit, which was well worth it. The plywood that it was made out of was basically birch. Howard Hughes hated the name Spruce Goose, but I guess the public and news media thought it sounded better than birch bird or birch goose.

Now we are off to Ginny's cousin, Carolyn, who lives in Tacoma, Washington. I really enjoyed our visit with them, though it was uneventful. We have reached our turn around, so we will be heading home.

Our next stop is to visit my neighbor's son, Adam, in Salt Lake City. That evening at supper, I tell him what he already knows—that his father is a minimalist and had given me an old train switching light that had been his grandfather's. I had really gotten the light from our other neighbor, Tony, who had been helping Tom clean out his father's property after he had passed. When he saw Tom throwing out the light, he stopped him, knowing that I would find a spot in my collection for it. Well, Adam had always liked that light, so I said that I would mail it to him so he could keep it in the family.

The following morning, we go to the top of the canyon's ski lift and have breakfast, never realizing we would be back in a couple of years to this spot for Adam's wedding. From here, we are off to Jackson Hole, Wyoming, for supper with an old sailing buddy, Roger from Boston.

The next morning, we cross the continental divide in a snowstorm, as we head for Rapid City, South Dakota. This is the state I reported on in high school and that I always wanted to go visit, but never thought I would get to do it, because it is such an out-of-the-way spot. As we cross into South Dakota, I have to stop in Sturgis to tell my biker buddies that I have been there and buy the proverbial Biker T-shirt. However, it's February—not August, when it's Biker Week. It is pretty quiet, but the wife chooses to stay in the Prius, while I have my beer in the Knuckles Saloon.

We get into Rapid City and the next morning, we head to Mount Rushmore. We almost can't see the presidents, because it is snowing pretty heavy again, but it finally lets up, so we get to see them. Then we head over to Crazy Horse, which if ever completed, could be considered the eighth wonder of the world. It will be 564 feet high and 640 feet long. The head is basically complete and it's 87 feet high. It is being done with no government monies, because admissions and donations are carrying the cost. It is a statue of a Lakota warrior and the Lakota people don't want any government funding. Some people think it will never be completed, but it is still very impressive as it sits there waiting to be finished. It is only 17 miles from Mount Rushmore. Two other major attractions in this area are the Jewell Caves and the Wind Caves. One other great advertised trip was to the Bad Lands, but they were not open due to bad weather (no pun intended).

Heading east, our next stop is Wall, aka Wall Drug—yes, the whole town is a drug store. It is said they first got people to stop for free water. The rest is history. Then off to Mitchell, its claim to fame being the Corn Palace. However, it's simply an arena they have taken and made a mural out of one wall with colored corn, which I grew up calling Indian corn. It is fantastic to see before the birds pick it clean. It has to be remade every three months, because not only do the people love it, , so do the birds.

It's hard for a guy who has grown up in a metropolitan area to see most of the exits on I-90 in this area are for private ranches. If they think the weather is going to get bad, these exits have gates that they just close up. You can be driving along with the sun out above you, but you cannot see more than fifty feet ahead of you. This is called a ground blizzard, which is caused by the wind blowing snow across the plains. The people here look at this weather like the people of Maine look at a fog bank. Yes, almost every part of the country has its own idiosyncrasy with weather.

My next stop is Chicago, Illinois, to visit the Tower that will always be the Sears Tower to me, even though they sold it to the Willis

Company. Having worked for Sears for thirty-four years, and being around for its conception in 1970, and for its completion in 1973, I always wanted to go up in it. It took 2,000 workers to complete the 110 floors and like everything else Sears touched, in later years it only filled about half of it. Then they sold it and developed Hoffman Estates as their corporate offices. I did enjoy going out in the glass room at the top, but later heard it had developed a crack in the floor that had to be repaired.

Now we are off to my youngest brother-in-law in Sandusky, Ohio. Yes, the seven-year-old when we got married is now forty-seven, and when we visited him, he had two sons and two grandchildren—yes, time does fly as the song goes, "Sunrise, sunset, quickly go the years."

For our last stop, we visit our niece at Rochester University in New York and have a very pleasant time before heading home. When the dust settled and the snowflakes melted, we had covered over 12,500 miles in three-and-a-half-months. Amazingly I still hear about places we missed, but I do not regret one minute of what we did see. I think that if you can afford it and you have your health, everybody should do this at least once in their life and the younger the better. Here it is now ten years later and I do not know if I could do it now, but I will never regret having done it. I do marvel at the people who just live on the road in their RVs. I missed five states, but had seen Alaska and Hawaii on other trips. I would see those last five states on a later trip, so then I could say that I had been to all fifty states.

I had a friend who sold his house and boat and took off with a twenty-four-foot RV. As time went by, he traded it for a thirty-foot RV. He said when he ended up in California, he went into an RV dealership with fifty sales people and he bought a thirty-six-foot RV.

When he comes home in the summer, he parks it in his daughter's yard until the road bug bites him again.

I have occasionally been asked what type of RV did I do this road trip in and get a strange look when I say a Prius. At Las Vegas, I did have to send through UPS two fifty-pound boxes back to the neighbors who were taking care of my mail. In New Mexico, we spent three hours testing wine and then we picked out two cases to be shipped home. When we gave the woman our address, I saw her almost collapse. She thought that her three hours of work had just gone down the drain. I asked what the problem was and she said that, at that time, we could not ship wine to Massachusetts. I asked if we could ship it to New Hampshire and she said yes, so we shipped it to our neighbor's daughter (problem solved).

My last thought on this road trip was that we stayed almost entirely in Best Westerns, because at the time, they had a catalog of all their units. What we would do as we traveled is we would figure where we would be in about four hundred to four hundred and fifty miles and almost always be able to find a Best Western within a fifty-mile range or window of our arrival. They have stopped printing this catalog, but thinking about this, I could still estimate where I would be for the next evening.

Their reasoning was they could not keep up with the pricing or whether the unit was still functioning, because Best Western sends people around to check to see if they are meeting B/W standards. If they find the unit substandard, they take away their franchise. This I have seen happen.

One time we had made our reservation, but when we got there, the motel said they did not have it. Probably we were booked at the motel at the other end of the mall. Yes, there were two in one strip mall. Being franchised, this can happen, though it is the only time I have seen it. We also stayed at B/W, because we got the equivalent of frequent flyer miles. Once, we charged our Platinum membership card, we were upgraded to a better room for the same price. We also saw this when we were traveling with my brother-in-law.

CHAPTER 19

Intercoastal Trip

When I get back from the road trip, I start thinking about this book and building a cabin down by my pond like Thoreau in nearby Lexington, Massachusetts. To write and watch the world go by in my senior years. To be closer to my geese and watch snapping turtles frolic and make little snapping turtles. This a sight everyone should get to see at least once.

I started building this cabin in my mind and found sleeping very hard while thinking about the cabin's construction. So I put the design down on paper and then figured out what I needed for materials and gradually got the cabin out of my head. A year later, my little cabin was complete—ten feet by twenty feet and two stories high. My friend, Jack, gave me a library ladder for Xmas to get to the second floor.

Now I have another bucket list that has to be taken care of. I had always wanted to go down the intercoastal waterway. I buy my charts, upgrade my chart plotter unit, and call my brother-in-law in Maryland to see if he is interested. He says yes and we leave from Rhode Island, where I had kept the boat the last three years in my old stomping grounds in Portsmouth, Rhode Island. We have to make it back in time for his daughter's wedding, just like I said we could.

The first place we stop is Block Island, Rhode Island, talking to a local. He asked where we were going and we say Maryland. He asked how we were going to get there and we said we planned to go through the East River. He told us we couldn't, because it is closed to all traffic, because of meetings at the United Nations. We told him about making Bill's daughter's wedding. He then tells us about a little known passage on the south side of Long Island. We could go through there.

He then told us there was one tricky tidal lock that only operated with the tides, but it was doable. We thanked him and saved a couple of days by following his recommendation. Keeping with the old adage, "Always talk to the locals and take their advice." We made the lock with the tide without a problem, but then come across a bridge that the charts say is a drawbridge, but it is not. After studying the chart, we find that this is an island with another bridge on the other side. When we go over to that side to look at the drawbridge, we find that it is marked as a fixed bridge. It seems all of the locals know of this error and think nothing of it, because this route is not really used as an intercostal passage. As a side note, the next time I am at this boat show, I will go to the Coast Gard booth and tell them of this error. When I did that later, they said they would report it, but I had to leave my name and show my ID. If I was wrong, they would get back to me. I never heard from them again. I have not seen a new chart, but I know it would have gone out as a notice to the mariner's monthly report.

Before getting started, I get in touch with Chuck; my old neighbor of many years ago. I ask him if he would still be interested in doing the intercoastal trip that we had talked about when we were in France on a riverboat cruise on the Seine. He said he would do Maryland to Florida. We make the arrangements for him to fly into Baltimore after the wedding. A couple of days after the wedding, we are off.

Chuck was in the navy for two years and when we saw the navy hospital ship, the Comfort, he said it was the first navy ship he had ever seen. How strange is that? He explained that he had been stationed on a naval air base in Texas, loading bombs on the under wings of jets.

At the end of the day, we cut through a small passage into a quiet little anchorage on the east side of the Chesapeake and spend our first night relaxing. The next morning, we head out on a different passage back onto the Chesapeake. We are taking pretty good waves on our starboard beam, because we have to stay in the channel and can't head into the waves. The boat is handling them well, but then I notice my black dog burgee is loose—the little flag is flying wildly on the bowsprit. I asked Chuck to take wheel while I go up and secure it. I could not take this trip without remembering MacDuff and Ebony.

We get back out on the Chesapeake and Chuck asks where the life preservers are. Perhaps I should have told him before we left, like I give instructions with my charters. Apparently when he took the wheel and saw me up on the bow, he was not sure if I was coming back. I tell him they are in the locker on the upper deck, but he asks, "What are they doing up there?"

I said, "That is the last place we would be before the boat went down." I don't think he liked that answer, so I said, "OK," and went up and got two life preservers for the main helm. His thought was that if I got washed over securing my black dog burgee, he would like to have a preserver next to him at the main helm. I could not argue with that logic.

After being with him a couple of days and him asking to repeat a lot of what I said, I realize Chuck is pretty deaf from loading those bombs under the wings of planes in Texas. The other thing that came up was when I gave him the helm and asked him to follow the red line on the chart plotter for the course. I go off to do other things and come back a little later to check on how he is doing. I see that we are not on the course I gave him. He points to another line that is *black* and says he is following the red one. It seems he is not only deaf, but color blind. We had a good laugh on this revelation and now I know I have to be clearer on my instructions.

When we get to Norfolk, Virginia, the marina we stay at has a pool docked in a slip and is floating. This is the first floating pool I had ever seen. Again, I guess it is my sheltered life.

The next day we pass three navy ships being built from the salvage metal from the World Trade Towers. These ships will go back to the Middle East to haunt them. Need I say more.

We then go to the beginning of the Great Dismal Swamp Canal. It sounds bad, but is really a lovely canal. Here we stop at a spot that is a rest area for Route 17 and a state pier for the boats transiting the canal. It is the oldest continually operating canal in the United States. Opened in 1805, it connects the Chesapeake Bay with Albemarle Sound, North Carolina, and was dug by slaves hired from nearby land owners. They started digging in 1793 and it was completed twelve years later. It is twenty-two miles long, six feet deep, and thirty-two feet wide. President George Washington agreed with the Governor of Virginia, Patrick Henry, that this would be the best way to bypass the treacherous North Carolina coast.

When we get to the rest area, we are able to tie up to the wall and as time goes by, other boats come along and raft to the inside boats. We end up with five boats long and four wide. After we're settled in, somebody from the rest area comes down and lets us know a storm is moving in from the west. We have to stay there, because at our next stop in Elizabeth City, North Carolina, which is full due to the storm. We ended up staying there for four days with no charge. We had a great time partying with new-found friends, almost all of us heading south.

I decide to drop my kayak in the water and paddle back down the canal a couple of miles. When I get back, Chuck (being the old navy man) is entertaining the people at the rest area who have walked down to see the strange collection of boats. I asked Chuck what he was doing and he said he was answering all their questions. I asked how he could do this and he simply said, "If they are asking the question, they don't know if my answers are right or wrong." As strange as this sounded, it made sense to me and we had a good laugh. We still talk about this stop as one of the highlights of the trip and always have a good laugh.

When we finally untie and sail into Elizabeth City, there is an old retired navy man helping everybody dock. A great meal was had by all and that morning, we are off to Dowry Creek Marina. It is now Halloween and we get invited to the Marina Halloween party. Almost everyone is there with their spouse. I always get a kick out of Chuck telling people we are not gay. I told him he really doesn't have to say it that way. Just say our wives don't like boating.

A sad thing about this marina was a fellow who had retired from the service. His goal and bucket list was to buy a marina on the Intercoastal Waterway. He talked his wife into pulling up their roots and burning all of their bridges up north, selling everything, and moving south. He got to live this dream and died in less than a year, leaving his wife to run the marina. She did have a couple that lived aboard to help her out and apparently, she had a son who had moved down to help her, also.

Outside the office was the first bottle tree I had ever run across. At the bottom of the bottle tree was the man's military plaque that the government makes up to put on a serviceman's grave. He was cremated and buried there. While writing this part, I called Chuck to ask his input and he gave me a couple of suggestions. Then he called me back the next day to tell me he had called the marina. They told him the lady had sold them the marina and she had taken her husband's ashes and plaque with her. They had also moved the bottle tree, but they invited us back.

When I got back home, I made a bottle tree in the man's memory. Not knowing his name, it is kind of my monument to the Unknown Soldier. When I moved, I brought my favorite bottles and now there are over one hundred bottles on it. And here is my bottle tree poem.

Bottle Tree

A bottle tree is a pillar of beauty
So simple in its utility
All shapes and colors
Giving tranquility for every fellow
Each bottle has a story if they could only speak to us
As we go through life without a fuss
A post of memories a bottle tree
Some have travelled far with me

White and clear, blue and brown
Red and green, from every town
They point upside down
While hanging quiet and calm
Some were poor, some were fine
Some held whiskey, some held wine
Some from the present, some from the past
All interesting shapes of glass
Plump and round, long and thin
I've saved them from the recycling bin
Their contents consumed for many reasons
To keep me warm or cool in all the seasons
Saw my first in Dowery Creek Marine
A tribute to a man I'd never seen
As time goes by
I hope it'll stay after I die

At the Halloween party, we met two guys that were moving a corporate yacht about eighty-five feet. They invited us over for a couple of drinks. We had a great time as my buddy, John, would say—swapping stories and telling lies and also seeing how the other half lives.

I always thought the Intercoastal Waterway was fairly protected, but I found both Albermarle and Pamlico Sound can pick up and get nasty. However, it is better than the Outer Banks where we took a hard knock.

What I had never thought of is going through Camp Lejeune. Here you have to make sure they are not firing or having training scrimmages. There is a stop and go light and when it is a go, it is with an escort to make this passage. As you go through, you see vehicles rolled over and tanks all around. It seemed slightly strange in this peaceful setting.

It was kind of uneventful from here to Jacksonville, Florida. We did pass some fantastic houses in basically marsh with the waterway passing through it.

I always find the dolphins fascinating, remembering a Paul Harvey story where, whenever it was really nasty and foggy, aka "Bill" (to use a name) would come out and lead a boat in for many years. Bill was a dolphin, who I remember lived in this area. He was part of life's journey to many people. When we get to Jacksonville, our guidebook mentioned a marina, so we decided to try it. As we are heading into it, we are overtaken by a Homeland Security patrol.

Apparently, this is a common place for illegals to enter into our country. We were not aware of this fact or that this marina did not have the best reputation—the guidebook did *not* mention this.

Security pulls up beside us and asks us where we were coming from and going to. We said we were coming from New England and we were going to Sanford, Florida. They also asked where we had spent the night. These were all good questions by folks just doing their job. I did not think of it, but before they boarded, the guy in charge notices my belt buckle. He then asked why it said "SAIL," while I'm at the helm of a power boat. I simply told him my last boat was a sailboat and old sailors never die—they just buy Trawlers. It seems this made sense to him. He said, "Thank you very much," and left without boarding us.

I have related this story to several friends in law enforcement and they say that if properly trained, these officers will have key questions to ask to find out if the person they are questioning is telling the truth and is on the up and up. That was his key question and so to this day, I can say that I have never been boarded.

What was strange was when we arrived at the marina, it seemed many of the boaters coming in had just abandoned their vessels. In the washroom was a table with about a six-inch pile of letters that had never been collected. This strange place seemed to be the end of the road for many people, so I could see why Homeland Security watched it.

Now it is time to go down one of the only northern flowing rivers in this country—the St. Johns. Our next stop is Green Cove Springs, where I used to live as child for half a year while my father was stationed here.

I had read an article on this old navy base. It was going to be made into a state-of-the-art marina, but had not happened just yet. As we head south, we enter Florida's largest lake, Lake George, and then into gator and manatee country.

This area of the St. John is really a strange waterway for an old Yankee. We end up at our destination in the Sanford Marina about ten miles from Chuck's house.

Now I fly back and get the wife and drive back. When we arrive, she informs me that we are not spending two months on the trawler, so we rent a condo.

We would go over and spend some time on the boat and occasionally, when friends come down, take trips up the St. Johns. This is the time I got together with Jack and went to visit Roger and Sue. They lived about eight miles from the boat.

We come down to the boat one day and see the lady on the boat next to us. Her husband was a helicopter mechanic in Asia and spent six weeks over there and six weeks at home. Now was his time to be over there. His wife tells us the story of her previous night. She had a sweetheart of a golden retriever, whom she had just brought out for his last bladder gladder trip for the evening. Bringing him back to the boat, he stops short and just starts to growl. She looks down into the dark and there is a black bear coming at them. She is able to get the dog back into the cabin and watches as the bear climbs around the security gate and goes about his way, but leaving a good clump of fur on the gate, which is still stuck there to back up her story. There were also stories of alligators basking in the sun on the swim platforms on the back of the boats. With all this going on, I know I would have had to rent the condo anyway.

There are people around Florida who like to go out and relocate nuisance alligators. However, the big bad ones that are attacking people get euthanized. A lot of them are brought to Lake Jessup. A tour boat goes out in that area and a restaurant right there serves gator four different ways. A Florida joke tells of a Seminole Indian being charged for killing a gator for food. The judge thinks it is legal and says he is going to his chambers to check the law. When he comes back, he tells the Indian he is free to go, but he asks him what gator tastes like. The Indian replies "Eagle."

At the end of our two months, we drive back. Then I fly out to meet with some friends from Boston, We bring the boat up to Jacksonville and they fly out, so I start my trip back to Maryland by myself. Teaming up with two other boats, I meet them every night for dinner and cocktails.

Now that we are back in Tewksbury, one of our neighbor's parents from Salt Lake City come to visit. Tom and Sue booked a dinner for us and Tony and Carol (our road trip mail service) to go to the Left Bank Restaurant in Tyngsboro, Massachusetts. It used to be called Silks, because it was also a retirement home for race horses.

Our dinner was a recreation of the last dinner of the Titanic. It was a ten-course meal and a glass of wine was served with each course, as it had been served on the Titanic. It was accompanied by a PowerPoint presentation on the ship's construction and features. This dinner was one of the most fantastic I have ever had. One of the courses was one oyster on the half shell—one of my favorite appetizers. My wife had never eaten one before, so I got her to try it and she really liked it. I think she did this to keep me from getting hers.

The rest of the summer was quiet and uneventful, so we start talking about going to Florida for the winter. Finally, we are off in November and stop at her brother's house outside of Lexington, Virginia. Going to Steve and Wendy's house is like taking a trip into the past. It is over one hundred fifty years old and constructed of chink logs like President Lincoln's first house.

Steve was a contractor, so one day he is looking for a customer's check that he had left on his desk. He searched for quite a while, but finally gave up for the moment. Before going to bed, he had a word with his resident ghost. He simply and sternly said, "George, put the check back," and then, he went to bed. The next morning, the check was back on the desk. I guess when your house is one hundred fifty years old, you have to live with ghosts. Being in the country, you also have to live with deer, aka brown cow, and bears. You cannot leave food on the porch and you must also have an eight-foot fence around your yard.

The first time I was there, I sat on the front porch reading a book.

The porch is close to the road that runs between Lexington and the Natural Bridge, but only three cars passed all day. That night, before I went to bed, I go outside and yell, "Good night, John Boy." Steve, having never had a television, so he had to ask my wife what was that all about.

Steve had several great dogs, Shanana, Lupine, and Bonnie. Shanana went everywhere with Steve. Lupine was just a regular dog and Bonnie was a true beagle. I loved to hike on the logging trails in back of Steve's cabin. One day, I am hiking along a trail, when I hear Bonnie off in the distance locked onto a scent, baying like a beagle. I stop and see her way down the trail, nose to the ground following some animals scent, ears to the wind, and running as fast as her little legs will carry her. She goes flying past me and stops about one hundred feet away. She turns and gives me a look like, "Oh, it was just you."

Bonnie, like Shanana and Lupine, are gone. They were all lucky dogs to have all those woods to run in. Steve tells the story of how sometimes Bonnie would come into the house filthy and smelling of dead deer. It seems she just loved to roll in a deer's carcass and then come in and lay under his stove to warm up.

Steve and Wendy's place is on twenty-seven acres. Across the street was a plot of land of about sixty acres for sale for $65,000. It was nice, but I could not live that far from the water. The people who bought it built a log farmhouse about eighty feet long with a farmer's porch and mounted four dormers on the roof. One of Steve's neighbors said it was nice, but she could not figure out why he put four dog houses on the roof.

I have been to a lot of great plays, seeing one every month for several years at the Merrimac Repertoire Theater in Lowell, Massachusetts. However, the best one was in Lexington, Virginia, played outside in an open-air pit.

It was about an old woman dying of cancer and a construction company closing in on her and building all around her property. She had a city girl as her hospice nurse—taking care of her with the construction noise in the background. The stage was basically a cutaway of her cabin. She was far wiser than the nurse, as she corrected the nurse on almost everything she did, from cooking to making a fire. Of all the plays I have seen, I have remembered this one almost entirely after twenty years.

Lexington, Virginia, is a college town with Washington and Lee University and Virginia Military Institute (VMI) nearby. This gives Lexington a very intellectual atmosphere.

CHAPTER 20

Florida Snowbirds

We finally make it to Florida to really begin our retirement years as snowbirds, aka people who can escape the winter's cold and snow. I asked my wife to pick out a spot using some of my reasonable criteria—no tourists and not crazy or crowded. This was tough, with Florida hosting most of those. However, what she found met all of those criteria and I could still reach the real Florida in less than an hour. One thing I did not mention was good hospitals and medical facilities (dentists and eye doctors). Our place is old Florida and so out-of-the-way that some people within twenty miles of it had not even heard of it. We ended up in Bokeelia, Florida, on Pine Island.

It is extremely hard to leave a place that you have been part of for forty years, but both my parents are gone and I'm an only child. Also, some of my friends and relatives have already headed south. This will be a test to see if we like it. Having been in all fifty states and there are so many great places, it is a big decision. I had been down to this area twenty-five years ago at Burnt Store Marina and golf course on a friend's boat. While I was there, I strolled into a real estate office to see what they had. It was all new on the island then and from the boat, it seemed like the middle of nowhere. I did leave my name and phone number, but I just felt it was too remote. Being smart salespeople, they called every three months for a couple of years. I dropped in not long ago to see how it turned out. It was nice and a little more developed, but it had a one-dog limit and we had our two Schnauzers.

One neighbor across the canal where we first rented was a fisherman. Every day when he returned with his boat and catch, he always had his buddy, a great blue heron, standing on his bow.

I am just getting used to life on Pine Island, aka Old Florida, when I pass a sign that says PIG farm in large letters. I thought this was strange, because I did not smell any pigs. We had one in Tewksbury and you could smell it for a couple of miles. As I got closer, I could see Pine Island Growers (PIG) on the bottom of the sign in small letters. They grow a huge amount of palm trees and ship them all over the world. The soil and weather here are perfect for growing palm trees and a variety of over six hundred palm trees are in this area. Pine Island grows about sixty different varieties and it does this in about half the time.

After renting for two months, we decide to buy a place of our own and become snowbirds, too. My wife gets on Zillow and starts the search. After about a week, I said, "Let's just go out and look around." So the search begins with our two little helpers, the schnauzers. We end up at a double-wide on a canal in St. James City at the other end of the island. I asked if she has ever been in a trailer and she says no. She goes into the open house and I stay out with the dogs, because it is illegal to leave dogs alone in a car in Florida. After about fifteen minutes, she comes out and says that we could bring the dogs into the double-wide. The way I like to tell the story is that the dogs liked it, so we bought it. This began our four years of snowbirding with our own place and the dogs traveled well. At one rest stop, there were two other couples with two miniature schnauzers. It was like a schnauzer dog show.

Pine Island has a CVS Drug Store, a veterinarian, a Winn Dixie supermarket, an Ace hardware store, a gas station, and several organizations: Elks, American Legion, VFW, and the Moose. Also, there is the Pine Island Boat Club and Matlacha Hookers (ladies fishing club that does a lot of charity work on the island). My wife has joined a book club and a ladies Bunko club (they play a dice game in groups of four), where twelve to sixteen ladies generally meet once a month. Along with all this, they have three large marinas and also twenty restaurants, some with biker bars, and one four-star restaurant. All this gives you something to do when you are bored.

Off Island are about sixteen miles of little shopping malls, restaurants, gas stations, Sam's Club, Walmart, and car dealerships. Within another ten miles are great beaches and at least two hundred other restaurants. In addition, several great hospitals and medical centers are available to handle all the retired seniors. This is to the southwest and I have only touched on a little bit of it. I forgot about the Southwest Airport, which connects to anywhere in the country and the Red Sox winter training camp at Jet Blue Park, which is a replica of Fenway Park, only a little newer (about 80 years newer).

About the third year we are down here, I go to have the Prius serviced. Not being one to just sit in a waiting room, I decided to go for a walk. One habit I never noticed that I had was that I sometimes walk with my hands in my pockets. As I am walking along, I pass over a raised panel of sidewalk from a protruding root, unlike New England, where it is a frost heave that does this. Not looking for a frost heave, I trip over it and go face down before I can break my fall with my hands. I don't know how long I was down, but when I come to, I brush myself off and head back to the dealership and wait for my car to be ready.

About five weeks after this incident, I go out with my eighteen-foot flats boat that had come with the double-wide. Coming back in, the wife comes out and asks what the problem is, because I could not dock the boat. From this time on, I do not remember anything. She tells me I really started acting strange, so she tries to get me into the car to bring me to the hospital. I am not agreeable to that and tell her I'm OK. She calls 911 and when they come to get me, my neighbors tell me I was waving at everybody like I was running for office, as they put me into the ambulance.

I come to about three or four o'clock the next morning with my hands tied to the bed and my head shaved. The doctor comes in and tells me I cannot raise my hands above my head. He then explains everything to me. My head had been bleeding for five weeks into my skull with no headache or pain, a condition he called a subdural hematoma and he had to drill nineteen holes in my skull to release the blood.

I am kept in intensive care for five days. When I finally get released to my wife, I cannot drive till I get a clean bill of health. I am kept under control for a month, until I finally get a release from my doctor, aka Doogie Hauser. When you get to be my age, all the doctors seem like they just got out of high school. He was a fantastic doctor and obviously knew all the latest techniques. He was probably in his thirties and I owe him my life, so I should not criticize how old he looked. The release form said he drained all the motor oil, at least, this is what it must have looked like. I was to have complete bed rest until I felt that I was back to normal.

One side effect of this whole thing is my memory has lost a little. I had started this book before my accident, but I had to put everything on hold for about a year. This being said, I still don't remember things at 100% and I have to ask my wife about some things. Now when I have a memory fart, I do not know if it is age, drink, or this fall. I am told it is all of the above.

I had Tom, who booked the Titanic dinner, watching the house in Tewksbury. One day I get a call about the time we had bought a regular house in Florida. He said that the toilets were all froze up and there was no heat in the house. We had installed a gas generator for any power failure while we were gone. The generator had not gone on when we lost power. The gas meter had failed, so the house had frozen up. We had fifteen splits in our forced hot water heating system. When we called the gas company explaining that the meter had failed, they said that they had gone around and tagged all the meters. If the meter failed, we should call them and they would come out and replace it. Their reply was that it was our fault, because we had not called them with notification of the failure and I did not have anybody checking the house. I told them I did not expect the person checking the house to see if the meter had been tagged as faulty. When I get home, I checked with all my neighbors to see if they had seen the notice on the meters and nobody had noticed this tagging. Fortunately, my insurance company paid the $30,000 bill and they sued the gas company and got their money back. I guess the corporate lawyers knew how to deal with the buffoonery of the gas company, so instead of replacing forty-year-old meters with a notice that their meters are ancient, they will replace them when they fail.

It was at this time I had to decide if I was going to bring the trawler back down to Florida or sell it, because I did not like the waters or the weather down here. I did keep my kayak, because this is some of the best kayaking in the country, if not the world, with mangroves and very shallow water. I regrettably sold the trawler.

When I have company, I like to bring them down to Everglades City and take them out on an airboat ride through the mangroves. They get up to about 40 mph and take corners at almost these speeds. Then they will swirl into lagoons and circle around. It is a thrill. One of the lagoons generally has raccoons in the trees looking for handouts and alligators looking for the raccoons to slip and fall into the water. Excitement of the deep south.

When we get back, I see a man driving his airboat up the ramp and onto his trailer in the parking lot. I mention this to our airboat captain. I said I had never seen an airboat driven onto a trailer like that. He said some of the guys would cover the bottom with Lucite and drive them on the roads. He related one story where a guy gets drunk and ends up flying down Route 29 with no lights at 3:00 a.m. and with the local sheriff sitting and waiting for customers. He takes off in pursuit and the airboat guy just laughs at him and takes off into a canal thinking he is home free. The sheriff gets the last laugh. He calls for a state police helicopter and they track him down in the swamp. He gets a heavy fine and loses his captain's license.

Florida has a lot of crazy stories. A guy breaks into a house and the police chase him into a canal. They find an alligator still chewing on a shoe. I googled crazy Florida stories and found that there is enough to support five or six authors. There is also a television station that has a crazy a Florida story almost every night and occasionally, they'll have a crazy story and preference it with, "This one is not from Florida."

CHAPTER 21

Good bye, Trawler/ Old House— Hello, New House

The trawler gets sold and I tell them I will fly up and help them move the boat to Buffalo, New York, where its new home will be. They say that's OK—they will ship it. After they find out how much it's going to cost them to remove the flybridge and ship the boat, they realize bringing it up the Hudson River and across the Erie Canal is a better option.

We take about five days to get it up to the beginning of the Erie Canal near Albany, New York. The new owner's wife comes to help him across the canal and I take a taxi to the Albany Airport with a taxicab driver that used to work at the Tarpon Lodge, less than a mile from my new home. I rented a car to finish my trip of four states. My first stop is Bill's in Marietta, Ohio. I stay with them a couple of days, then it's off to finish my tour of four states that I had not seen: North Dakota, Nebraska, Colorado, and Kansas. In my travels, I get to see a couple of places I had missed on my road trip. The *Field of Dreams* near Dyersville, Iowa, and one of my favorite TV shows, *Pickers*, in LeClair, Iowa, on the History Channel, as well as, Ike's home town in Abilene, Kansas.

After I'm home, I look back at all the times I had moved with my parents and thought nothing about it—just shows how resilient a child is to change. Selling my old house in Tewksbury, Massachusetts, and moving to the new one in Bokeelia, Florida, was monumental.

Packing up forty years of stuff is in itself overwhelming. My friend Tom, aka Booker of the Titanic dinner, is a minimalist. I admire him for this quality. This is the guy that was throwing out his father's switching light that Tony saved and gave to me, which I mailed to his son.

My wife calls me a hoarder, but my philosophy is three of anything is a collection. Three collections are a museum. I am the curator of my museum—not a hoarder. You can walk around in my museum. Though in her defense, after the movers weighed our load on Interstate 95, they asked me, "Do you realize you just shipped 20,000 pounds of stuff?"

In my defense I could not just throw out everything, without going over it. I also find it very hard to get rid of a lot of my parents' stuff. Being an only child, I have an extreme sentimental value to my parents' things that they found dear to them. I cannot divide this among my siblings.

I thought I did pretty good filling three dumpsters and parting with my 700 *National Geographic* magazines before we moved.

I knew where everything was in the old house, but when I want something now, I frequently cannot find it or sometimes I find things I forgot I had, while looking for something else.

I should also admit my love of scotch has probably taken its share of brain cells. I generally have fifteen to twenty different scotches in my bar and some you cannot even buy in the states, one being Ben Nevis, which to Scotsmen is the best and they do not let the good stuff out of the country commercially. However, a tourist is allowed two bottles and I have toured the whisky trail three times. I did not spell whisky wrong—the Scotts do not have an e in whisky.

A fascinating thing I learned in a Johnny Walker seminar is Johnny Walker Blue does not have an aged number of years on the bottle—being a blend, it has to have the youngest age of the blend. Some five-year old's can be fantastic and used in the blue blend, so they would have to put five years on the bottle. Nobody is going to spend $160 for a five-year-old blended Scotch, so they omit it. I was in a fine restaurant once and on the liquor selection, they had Johnny Blue twenty-five-year-old. I asked the waiter if I could see the bartender, so he sent him over and I nailed him on this error.

Another strange story is Johnny Walker King Arthur Scotch that can sell for $400 to $500 is simply a blue in a crystal bottle and when somebody hits big in a casino, the scotch that comes out of that crystal bottle is $150 and it is really a blue that should be sold for $50—the person does not get the crystal bottle. I cannot positively say this is correct This is just one of those stories I put a disclaimer on, if it was word of mouth, but I thought was right.

These prices are just arbitrary. When I went on a Hawaiian cruise, the Johnny Walker Blue sold for $12.00 a shot and at the end of the cruise, I go to my favorite bar and the bartender says, "I'm sorry, Mr. Flagg, but you have depleted the ship's stock." I did not have a problem with some five-year-old scotch being in my drink. The ship's stock was probably a couple of bottles. My pricing is only for examples and I could be way off on what the prices actually are. Like the example I gave remembering when we got gas for water skiing for .12 cents a gallon back in the mid-fifties. A draft beer in Boston can be six to twelve dollars. In St. James City in Florida it is two dollars and fifty cents. I always feel like a big spender when I buy somebody a drink on Pine Island. Everything is relative.

When I first went to Scotland in 1970 on my honeymoon, there were around eighty different distillers, but now there are about one hundred twenty to one hundred thirty distillers. Many of these are putting out three to six different labels and I know Johnny Walker is putting out ten to twelve. There are volumes of books about this subject. I have really digressed but I do enjoy reading some of my books on Scotch. One final thought is that all this Scotch is aged in bourbon barrels from the south that are only used once to age the bourbon, then shipped to Scotland. I had never thought about it, but they do not ship empty barrels. They break the barrels down and ship them unassembled with coppers and reassemble them in Scotland and repairing them if needed. This was as interesting a tour as a distillery on the whiskey trail.

I am not much on bourbon, gin, tequila, or vodka. They all have complicated stories that go with their quality, taste, and history. However, I do have one story about vodka. It seems that when Volks Wagon came to the American market, it was considered Hitler's people car and did not go over well, so they hired an advertising agency that came up with several things that helped. So Smirnoff hired Milton Goodman of the Lawrence C. Cumbinner Agency to help their lackluster vodka sales and Milton simply came up with, "It leaves you breathless." The rest is history. Milton recently died at 102. I do not know if he liked vodka.

CHAPTER 22

Getting Used to Florida

One of my neighbors use to say, "The joys of being a land baron," as we worked on our yards. Florida property is completely different than Massachusetts property. The biggest difference is up north, when the leaves fell in October, you raked them up, and you were done with them. In Florida, palms spit out fronds all year long, to the point that they actually have a vegetation truck come around every week, plus every other flora that is trying to consume the yard. I saw a TV show that did a time lapse on what would happen if you just let nature run its course, using a section of Detroit as an example. It is amazing how fast things can be overrun.

Grass grows in the rainy season, which is not very long. When I come down full-time, I hire a neighbor's friend from the double-wide to cut my grass. He would come every couple of weeks and if it needed cutting, he would do so and send a bill for $35. There would be times he would just drive by and if it did not need cutting, he would just keep going. This worked well for a year. Then he had a heart problem and sold the business.

The fellow that bought it came every week, sometimes just making one swipe in the front yard and one swipe in the back. This took all of five minutes and I'd get a bill for $35 every week, which was getting to be a little annoying. Then a hurricane came and my neighbor hired a guy to come in and clear her trees, so I hired the same fellow. He took down all my fallen trees for $600.

When the lawn guy comes, he asked what the tree guy had charged and I told him. He said, "That's high." When I'm not home, he comes and asks my wife if she wants the trees in the front trimmed. When she says OK, he does about half the work of the tree guy and charges $600. Then he has the nerve to ask who my financial accountant is, if this was too much.

I go out and buy a lawn mower, so the next time he comes, I tell him, "Don't bother coming back, because I needed the exercise." When I first came down, my neighbor at the double-wide warned us to watch out for some people around here, because they will take advantage of you any time, they think they can get away with it. He was right.

Gardening down here is different, since most of the soil is sand. Apparently, this part of Florida was under water a long time ago. I have not been able to grow much because of the soil or the heat. I have taken a couple of coconuts and planted them and my neighbor told me how to grow pineapples. I really miss my garden from up north.

CHAPTER 23

Pine Island

The local supermarket is Winn Dixie. All the buffoons that want to tear down the statues and change the south's history want Dixie out of the supermarket's name. And for some reason, they do not want the capital of Ohio to be called Columbus. I digress!

Where I was going with this story was in the supermarket parking lot up by the road, you used to be able to put your car, RVs, boats, and trailers or anything else you wanted to sell and sell it. One day I see a 2005 Mustang convertible for sale. I had been thinking about a ragtop for a while, having owned three in the past. I thought it was not right to be down in Florida without one. I can be kind of impulsive, so I now have a brown pony to ride around Pine Island in—my other convertibles were a 1959 black Chevy, a 1963 maroon Chevy, and the one I miss the most, a 1961 four-passenger brown Mercedes Benz cabriolet. The strange thing about the 1959 Chevy was its fins. If I came over a rise doing more than sixty miles per hour, I could become airborne. I heard that when California State Police bought 1959 Chevies, they had to replace them, because they could not keep them on the ground on high-speed pursuits. This one I could not confirm on Google and it is only a memory, but I am sure I am right on this. Google did confirm the fact, which I knew, of the 59s going airborne, but did not mention the California Highway

Patrol having a problem with the design.

I have always been a joiner of organizations. I believe it is a great way to meet people and almost all organizations have a charitable cause. It is also a great way to get the pulse of a community.

I just received my fifty-year pin from the Masons and have been in the Power Squadron for over forty years. The Power Squadron's goal is to teach safe boating as a national organization. The Masons are a charitable organization that take care of their own. With two higher branches, the Scottish Rite that helps the community, and the Shriners that take care of children that have had serious burns or who have lost limbs or have been born without them. These organizations do not charge for their care and when joining, you are brought to, in my case, Boston Shriners Hospital to meet the children you are helping. You cannot forget their smiling faces as they lay there with serious burns.

I have talked to many people in numerous organizations. Almost all of them say it is hard to get young people to join and help in any charity work. I guess I'm getting to be an old fart, when all I see is, iPhone and computer zombies.

In keeping with my joiner philosophy, I have joined the Sons and Daughters of the American Legion in memory of my father. I joined the Pine Island Boat Club to meet people that share my interests. Also, the Elks and the Moose—these last two I told the wife I should really have both sets of horns. All these organizations are charities in one form or another. Other charities I support are St. Jude and Boys Town. I feel bad not giving to the other thirty-five that have my address. The problem is that they all want $15 to $35. I have done the math and if I tried to support all of them, I would become one of their charities.

When I had a land line up north, I tracked the charities that were calling on the phone, which can be very annoying. I realized that the people that are calling are simply doing their job. When I got a call, I thought it was rude to hang up on those people, even though they generally called at suppertime, because they knew when you would be home.

So like them, I had a prepared text to read to these callers. I simply explained that I knew they doing their job, but I could not afford to give to all of the organizations that called me. Then I would say these are the people that have called and start to read the list of all fifty. I did not feel badly about hanging up on them, because they would all hang up on me before I got to the fifth charity.

Now you get a robocall that turns you over to a real person to take your money if you are inclined. Another problem is most of the money that is sent to these organizations goes to the corporate payroll. (Tom Lehrer was a satirical folk singer. One-of his songs goes, "If you did not enjoy the song, you should never let begin.") I have digressed.

After having been down here for ten years part- and full-time, I have become a local. I was not aware of this until I walk into one of my watering holes and sit down. My drink has already been put where I always sit. The guy sitting next to me asks, "Who are you?" This sounded like a strange question. He then tells me he had been trying to get a drink for fifteen minutes.

A couple of years ago, I decided to walk the length of Pine Island (seventeen miles) and it took a several days to do it. There are two public water fountains along the way—any other mention of watering holes will be or have been about adult beverages.

There are about twenty adult watering holes, give or take with the economy, each entirely different on the island. One is Bert's, which is really off the island by about five hundred feet from the bridge, but is considered part of the island. It has a steel pan player (Skip Elliott Bowman). He is one of the most interesting guys I have met down here and I am simply going to give you his bio.

Skip got his start in his music career at age four in Portland, Oregon, singing on a local TV show: *Talent on Parade*. After taking lessons on piano and cello, Skip went on to teach himself upright bass, saxophone, guitar, drum kit, trumpet, bush guitar, French horn, shakuhachi [Japanese bamboo flute], tuba, trombone, vibes, marimba, flugelhorn, bouzouki, and baritone.

Skip has played across Europe and the United States (including Carnegie Hall and Lincoln Center in New York City), Canada, Mexico, the South Pacific, and the Caribbean. In 1998 he taught himself steel pan and pays regular visits to the West Indies to research, collect, and play music.

In his spare time, Skip is a published writer and photographer for international travel magazines. He also adds that he is deeply in love with his wife, Margit.

Many times, when I pick people up at the airport, I will stop at Bert's to set the mood of the island with Skip's music that he calls steel pan. However, I had always known it as steel drums and I always ask him to play my favorite song, *Yellow Bird*.

My other two favorite watering holes are about an eighth of a mile apart in St. James City, but they are completely different. The first is very tropical and has a tiki hut roof and is completely open air. It has a more reserved clientele. Several reasons I like it here is because the food is over the moon and they have Guinness on draft. I have given them three things that fit more here than in my house down here. So I feel more at home while sitting there. The bartenders no matter how busy or how many there are never bump into each. When the chef rings the bell, somebody picks up the order up within ten seconds most of the time to give to the customer, no matter who took the order.

Another thing I find fascinating is all the bar/restaurants on the water have dockage without any charge. The restaurants in New England charge $5 to $10 an hour to tie up to eat. Also, in almost any bar/restaurant you can start up a conversation with the person next to you simply by asking, "Where are you from?" I find this really easy, having been to all fifty states, to have a conversation. Rarely will you find anybody who has grown up here.

The other watering hole says it all—the Ragged Ass, sometimes followed by the Dive Bar. I spend a little more time here, because most of the clientele are truly locals (like myself more than ten years). One day somebody introduced me as a local. I liked that. This place is far stranger than the Low Key. It has a much larger biker crowd and some days are entirely different than others. I was talking with one of my double-wide neighbors and asked him (being a biker) what he thought one of the bikes was worth. He said, "I don't know, but I'll find out." He came back in about ten minutes and said, "$65,000."

A lot of the guys have worked what I call normal jobs all their lives—bankers, cops, firefighters, lawyers, managers, and were never able to be the tough-looking biker they wanted to be. After they retired, they grow their beards and long hair. Their true inner personalities have been able to surface. This being said, the greetings are fist bumps and hugs for the retired pussy cats. I have been going to the Ragged Ass for ten years and I have never seen one confrontation, although I'm sure there have been some. As I get to know them, most all have had very interesting lives and are from all over the country. One guy was from California and this puzzled me, so I asked him why he ended up here. His answer made sense—the climate and the cost of living—the same reasons I was down here.

I like to read a lot of local authors. One book was *The Popping Cork Murders*. It took place on Pine Island and mentions the Ragged Ass. Matt is one of the people it mentions and it describes him as having a full bushy beard down to his chest. I think of Matt as the Ragged Ass greeter, because he does this so well, knowing most people by name. I asked if he was the greeter in this book and he says yes. I told him that if it was my book, I would have called him Gator. It seems he had grown up in the Everglades. He has a great tattoo on his bicep of a gator.

Dennis is another fellow I enjoy talking to and getting the news from Key West. He makes the three-hundred-mile trip twice a week supplying restaurants. There are about twenty people who are truly locals and another twenty that are not there when I am.

Another strange thing about the Ragged Ass is the vehicles that people come in or on. Golf carts are a very normal form of transportation for locals with their doggies, huge flags with their political preference or just the American flag, and even an occasional Confederate flag. Motorcycles of all vintages and sports cars, antique cars or classics cars are also being used. One day a picnic table with a tiki hut top, a beer keg for a front bumper (with tap), and a steering wheel in the table pulls in.

Max is not able to visit like he used to, because he moved to the center of the island and his transportation is a tricycle. We were talking about my pool table (it seems this was his profession, working with pool tables) and I said it was bigger than a standard table. He said it was still a standard table as long as the inside length was twice the width. I have talked with a lot of people in the fifty-seven years I have owned the table and nobody ever knew that. The name of the table company is Briggs and Son. Here he said that Briggs became Brunswick around 1860. I had never been able to date the age of the table before this. This puts the table at least 160 years old and possibly older. The guys who put the table back together said all the serial numbers on the frame were the same. That makes it more valuable, because when a pool hall was closed and the tables were broken down, the tables just ended up in piles and the serial numbers of the frames went every which way. This table stayed as a complete original. I weighed the table as each piece was assembled and it came out to almost exactly 1,000 pounds. I asked the last fellows that assembled it for me if they could order new leather pockets. They said sure. When they came back to install them, they said they had never seen a table like it in twenty years and just before they got the new pockets, they had seen one like it in Fort Myers. It too was from the Boston area.

The Ragged Ass has several handymen. The electrician had been a go-to guy for bands in Las Vegas. His flow of energy I would call a coiled spring, but he is a good coiled spring.

Another fellow comes up to me and asked if I am still in Bokeelia and I say yes, thinking I recognized him, but could not place him. After he left, it came to me that he was the guy who put in my double-wide's new floor. When I bought the house, I told the real estate agent that the survivors had told me that that the fence on the left was three feet over on my neighbor's property. He was the guy who moved it. I had not recognized him, because he had changed his modified Mohawk hairdo.

The Ragged Ass draws crowds with their music and the Low-Key draws crowds with their fund-raising events. One of these events is the Zero K marathon, because the bars are next door to each other. You start at the Low Key and you "run" to Woodie's next door doing challenging things like flipping bicycle tires instead of truck tires and cross a balance beam two inches by eight inches that is lying on the ground and you are given a rope to hang onto while doing this. The other event is the Great Rubber Duck race. They drop about 3,000 numbered ducks in the canal. You buy a ticket for a duck for $5. The first duck across the line wins $500. There is a $20 ticket that I think pays $1,000. These ducks are bigger. The money from these two events goes to the Calusa Land Trust to buy up property on the island to keep developers from overcrowding it. They put the land into parks and preserves for the local fauna.

Some unusual things about our new home is it is less than a mile from Calusa oyster mounds like those I visited in Maine on the Damariscotta River just north of Booth Bay. These were not the same native Americans, but the mounds or mittens were formed about the same time and used the same process for disposing of oyster shells.

I'm about three miles from Cabbage Key and Jimmie Buffet's cheeseburger in Paradise by the way the crow (or in this case, seagull or osprey) flies. It seems Jimmie was staying here in the seventies and had a perfect cheeseburger with a cold beer and piano after an awesome day of fishing. Then he wrote this song for his album, *Son of a Sailor Man*. I have had their cheeseburgers and they are awesome.

When I first moved here, I planted a lemon tree and I had an unplanned bucket list accomplished. I made my own lemon-drop martini from my own lemons. I still have to say that the best lemon-drop martini I have had was at McGarvey's Saloon in Annapolis, Maryland, by a bartender I'm told gave Walter Cronkite's eulogy. That brings to mind the time I'm sitting in the cockpit of my sailboat and my brother-in-law is using binoculars to watch a fellow sail into Martha Vineyard's harbor. He is sailing into a bunch of small sailboats on their moorings. He turns to me and says, "This guy is either crazy or he really knows what he is doing." As the boat sails safely past, I see that the guy at the helm with a huge smile on his face is Walter. He really knew what he was doing!

CHAPTER 24

Hemingway

Now that I live in Florida year-round, I'm able to go down to Key West and enter the Hemingway look-alike contest. It is around the 21st of July, which was his birthday. Having lived up north, I never took the time to come down for it. Now, living a couple hundred miles away, I can drive there in six hours or take the fast ferry out of Fort Myers in three hours.

It seems like Key West has an event every month. One of the strangest is their Fantasy Feast. I will not go into the details of this event. It does not get as much press as Mardi Gras, but from what I have seen online, I think it rivals that celebration. It also has a film festival, so I went online to see what each month has for a festival. I found out what they call each event and that there is one almost every week. They have to have an incredible Chamber of Commerce.

I never thought about looking like Hemingway, but people started telling me I should compete. My friend and intercoastal buddy, Chuck, was the first one to mention this to me. Then several people at the Ragged Ass mentioned it, too. Then people I just passed on the street started calling me Ernest or Hem. In Cuba, at Hemingway's favorite watering hole (El Floridito), the habaneros started calling out "Ernesto, Ernesto."

I did not know what to expect from the look-alike contest. The event takes place at Sloppy Joes on Douval Street. The first time I was there, they took eighty people each night for two nights and they give each contestant a half to one minute to plead their case. Out of these, they choose fifteen people each night. Then, on the third night they have thirty people and from this group, they choose the papa for that year. You are probably wondering who "they" are. They are the winners from previous years.

This tourist attraction is strange in itself, because people will just buy you drinks and ask if they can take a picture of you with their kids. They will also dress their dogs up with gray beards, bandannas, and red berets.

While I'm sitting there enjoying this whole event, I hear that there are guys competing from New Zealand and Sweden. What is really funny is sitting around and having a beer with everybody that looks just like you from all over the world. It is like a fun house mirror. I happen to mention that I heard one of the guys is from New Zealand. Everyone has a good laugh and points to the guy sitting next to me.

Hemingway was a huge fan of the Spanish bull fights. He even had several bull fighters as friends. He wrote what is considered the best book ever on bull fighting (*Death in the Afternoon*), which I read and found fascinating, since about a third of it was about the bull fighters, another third was pictures of the moves and stances, and the last part is a glossary of the moves, stances, and terminology of bull fighting.

The reason I mention this, is that part of the event is the running of the bulls through Key West, like in Palermo, Spain. It is not what you are thinking. Where do they get the bulls? They have saw horses and put horns, saddles, and wheels on them and push them around the block. Tell me this is not strange.

Winning is not important to me, but that being said, I would not mind winning. The really great thing is the money raised goes to a college in Key West.

I could not afford to live in Key West, but I do enjoy going there a couple of times a year. There is so much to see and do there, such as Harry Truman's Winter White House, Mel Fisher's Treasure Museum, and the many art stores along Douval Street. Other great things to do are sailing trips to the Dry Tortugas and visiting excellent restaurants everywhere, in addition to walking along their fantastic beach. Also, I can't forget Mallory Square at sunset. As the evening looms, it almost looks like zombies are drawn to this magical spot. Many street performers gather there, but the main attraction is the sunset.

I was entertaining my brother and sister-in-law and brought them to a good viewing spot, explaining that a green flash could be witnessed here. As we are standing there, I see a schooner heading to the point of sunset and thought it was going to block the view. It didn't make it in time, so yes, I witnessed the green flash! I looked at my brother and ask if he saw it, too. He just smiled. The green flash (and rarely called the green ray) is a metallurgical optical phenomenon that sometimes occurs transiently around the moment of sunset or sunrise. When conditions are right, a distinct green spot is briefly visible above the upper rim of the sun's disc. When the green appears, it usually lasts for no more than two seconds. This is *Wikipedia*'s explanation.

I have been a boater all my life and heard of the green flash probably for fifty years. I knew it existed, because I have talked to many boaters about it. One of the stories was about a friend of mine who knew a pilot that had actually followed the sunset in a jet and watched it for about four to five seconds.

One person I talked to about the flash worked at an outside bar in Key West looking out onto Mallory Square. I asked him how long he had been a bartender there, and he said for about sixteen years. I then asked the big question. "Have you ever seen the green flash here?"

His answer, "Twice!" He told me once was a normal sunset. The other was when a famous singer was going out to disperse the ashes of one of his band members, who had committed suicide over a broken romance. The bartender caught the green flash between boats in a procession of about fifty boats.

After moving to Florida and competing in the Hemingway look-alike event, I started to study his life and read many of his books. There are some that are not in the library or are out of print, but I have read perhaps twenty out of about thirty he has written.

I have found his stories deep and complicated for an uneducated person like myself, with a frequent mention of the liquor, absinthe. I looked up this drink in my cocktail book and I quote from the field guide to cocktails, "Absinthe is a strong herbal liqueur distilled with many flavorful herbs, including licorice, hyssop, anise, veronica, fennel, lemon balm, angelica, and wormwood." Although true absinthe is illegal, contemporary manifestations, which have an anise flavor, are quite popular. Every historian of nineteenth-century literature and art knows that absinthe was a veritable poison.

Suicide was Hemingway's demise on July 2, 1961 in Ketchum, Idaho. There is a great deal I could write about the man after studying what he has written and the volumes that have been written about him. I will say it has given me many hours of enjoyment in my retirement and I am going to leave it at that.

Hemingway actually lived in Cuba longer than any other place. Finca Vigia (meaning look-out farm) is an aptly named setting up on a hill overlooking Havanna Harbor. He was there for twenty-two years and left when Castro took power. They only met once for a fishing tournament and contrary to popular belief, there was no love lost there. I was able to visit there during a very short window of time for US tourism on a cruise ship in 2019.

It was an interesting trip and the people were wonderful. The government is screwed up, but it has been so for its entire five-hundred-year history. Going to Cuba is a trip back into time. Everybody knows about their antique cars that are 1959 vintage or older. Most people are not aware of the fact that there are 6,000 cars on the island. When you get close to them, you can see almost all are being held together by bondo and a prayer. Their engines are mechanical miracles, running with boat motors, old Russian car engines, and with very good mechanics rebuilding the existing engines.

The people are very proud and they try to keep the facades of their buildings looking nice. However, when you look down the sides of the buildings, you see that a lot of them are crumbling down.

I went out to a world heritage site on a tour bus on a four-lane highway. The tour bus we were in was doing 50 mph, as we were passing donkey-drawn carts. We stopped at a tobacco farm, where a farmer is demonstrating how to roll Cuban cigars. After the demonstration, he handed out cigars for us to try with a shot of Cuban rum, which was delicious. The cigars were a dollar (or the equivalent). I tried to buy a bottle of the rum , but he said no—wait there. He came back with a bottle that he hands to me. I ask, "How much?"

He said, "It is yours. My gift to you, because Hemingway has been good for my business and you look so much like him." Like I say, the people of Cuba are wonderful. We also stopped at a rest area for a potty stop. The women were forewarned to bring toilet paper or they would have to buy it.

A big tree outside the rest area hung all the way to the ground. People would climb under its limbs and leaves and come out with packages. From talking to people about what I witnessed, I think it was a black market for what was not available on the open market. This is only an assumption.

The World Heritage site was a limestone cliff about 900 feet long by 250 feet high with primitive paintings on it. I have never seen anything like it and had never heard of it, but it was definitely worth the trip.

Cuba's ports are closed again to tourist trade with the United States. I am not sure who closed on who. I tried to google this question and all I interrupted was political speak. It is a shame that politics has to be so messy, what with Cuba being only ninety miles away from Key West.

Reading about Key West, I learned about a business that made it wealthy. In an excellent book called *The Gulf* by Jack E. Davis, which says that around 1850, salvage outfits operated under a license issued by the Federal Court. Journalist, Hunter S. Thompson described it as the "cruel imperatives of salvaging rights." This meant whoever got to the cargo first and could defend it with any form of weapon or sheer strength had rights to it. These people were called wreckers, because they would tear down any navigational aids and put up phony light signals to cause a wreck.

After Flagler put in a railroad and the government put in a highway, Key West has been a magnet for any tourist looking for something exotic and different. The wealthy can enjoy a fantastic lifestyle year-round in this location.

In Closing

Life's journey is not over, but is nearing its end. And I'm coming into my harbor. Some of my friends have already sailed on.

One of my friends, Jack, passed recently, so I called his wife, to see how she was doing. She said their kids and grandchildren were keeping her busy. We talked about how Jack loved to cook breakfast for all his kids on Sundays. I remembered this, but then she also told me that on Thanksgiving Day, he liked to bake a pumpkin pie.

Then she mentioned that she goes to his grave often. That's why she recently noticed that a pumpkin was growing beside his tombstone. Since Thanksgiving was coming, she was checking with everyone to find out who might have planted the pumpkin. Nobody knew who might have done it.

I smiled as I told her, "I do!" Jack was a gardener!

Photo Gallery

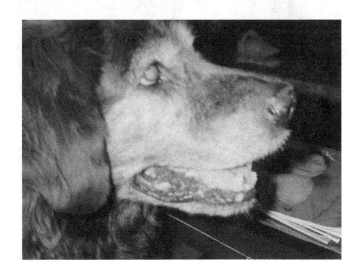

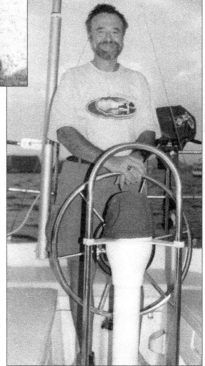